SPIRITUALITY
in
EDUCATIONAL
LEADERSHIP

D0958224

The Soul of Educational Leadership

Alan M. Blankstein, Paul D. Houston, Robert W. Cole, Editors

THE SOUL OF EDUCATIONAL LEADERSHIP

VOLUME 4

SPIRITUALITY
in
EDUCATIONAL
LEADERSHIP

PAUL D. HOUSTON ❧ ALAN M. BLANKSTEIN ❧ ROBERT W. COLE

EDITORS

A JOINT PUBLICATION

CORWIN PRESS
A SAGE Company
Thousand Oaks, CA 91320

For information:

Corwin Press
A SAGE Company
2455 Teller Road
Thousand Oaks, California 91320
www.corwinpress.com

SAGE Ltd.
1 Oliver's Yard
55 City Road
London EC1Y 1SP
United Kingdom

SAGE India Pvt. Ltd.
B 1/I 1 Mohan Cooperative
   Industrial Area
Mathura Road, New Delhi 110 044
India

SAGE Asia-Pacific Pte. Ltd.
33 Pekin Street #02–01
Far East Square
Singapore 048763

Printed in the United States of America.

Library of Congress Cataloging-in-Publication Data

Spirituality in educational leadership/edited by Paul D. Houston, Alan M. Blankstein, and Robert W. Cole.
        p. cm.—(The soul of educational leadership ; v. 4)
"A joint publication with the Hope Foundation and the American Association of School Administrators."
Includes bibliographical references and index.
ISBN 978-1-4129-4941-5 (cloth)
ISBN 978-1-4129-4942-2 (pbk.)
    1. Educational leadership—Psychological aspects. 2. School management and organization—Psychological aspects. 3. Educational leadership—Moral and ethical aspects. 4. School management and organization—Moral and ethical aspects. 5. Spirituality. I. Houston, Paul D. II. Blankstein, Alan M., 1959- III. Cole, Robert W., 1945- IV. Hope Foundation. V. American Association of School Administrators. VI. Title VII. Series.

LB2805.S7424 2008
371.2—dc22   2007029939

This book is printed on acid-free paper.

07   08   09   10   11   10   9   8   7   6   5   4   3   2   1

Acquisitions Editor:	Elizabeth Brenkus
Managing Editor:	Allyson P. Sharp
Editorial Assistants:	Ena Rosen, David Andrew Gray
Production Editor:	Cassandra Margaret Seibel
Copy Editor:	Teresa Herlinger
Typesetter:	C&M Digitals (P) Ltd.
Proofreader:	Wendy Jo Dymond
Indexer:	Joan Shapiro
Cover Designer:	Michael Dubowe

CONTENTS

ACKNOWLEDGMENTS

W e wish to express our gratitude to those Corwin staff members who serve as our lifeline on this project: Allyson Sharp and Lizzie Brenkus, our superb editors; David Gray and Ena Rosen, their on-top-of-everything editorial assistants; Astrid Virding, who continues to coordinate the daunting task of turning a book's worth of manuscripts into a book; and Teresa Herlinger, who catches anything the rest of us miss. Without their unfailingly patient, knowledgeable work, there would be no *Soul of Educational Leadership* series. All of us are in their debt.

We also wish to express our deepest gratitude to our dozens of contributors. As this series grows in length and breadth, we are humbled by the wealth of deep knowledge and experience brought to this enterprise by dozens of talented, committed educators who have consented to join forces with us. We are merely channeling their life-changing work. Without them, truly this series could not hope to exist.

Corwin Press gratefully acknowledges the contributions of the following individuals:

Jennifer Baadsgaard, Assistant Principal for Curriculum
Roosevelt High School
San Antonio, TX

Kermit Buckner, Professor
Department of Educational Leadership
East Carolina University
Greenville, NC

Kimberly Gruccio, Principal
Egg Harbor Township High School
Egg Harbor Township, NJ

Lila Jacobs, Professor and Coordinator
Urban Leadership Program
California State University, Sacramento
Sacramento, CA

Kenneth Killian, Assistant Professor
Vanguard University of Southern California
Costa Mesa, CA

Paul Young, Past President, National Association
    of Elementary School Principals
Executive Director
West After School Center, Inc.
Lancaster, OH

ABOUT THE EDITORS

Paul D. Houston has served as Executive Director of the American Association of School Administrators since 1994.

Dr. Houston has established himself as one of the leading spokespersons for American education through his extensive speaking engagements, published articles, and his regular appearances on national radio and television.

Dr. Houston served previously as a teacher and building administrator in North Carolina and New Jersey. He has also served as assistant superintendent in Birmingham, Alabama, and as superintendent of schools in Princeton, New Jersey; Tucson, Arizona; and Riverside, California.

Dr. Houston has also served in an adjunct capacity for the University of North Carolina, Harvard University, Brigham Young University, and Princeton University. He has served as a consultant and speaker throughout the United States and overseas, and he has published more than 100 articles in professional journals.

Alan M. Blankstein is Founder and President of the HOPE Foundation, a not-for-profit organization whose honorary chair is Nobel Prize–winner Archbishop Desmond Tutu. The HOPE Foundation (Harnessing Optimism and Potential through Education) is dedicated to supporting educational leaders over time in creating school cultures where failure is not an option for any student. HOPE sustains student success.

The HOPE Foundation brought W. Edwards Deming and his work to light in educational circles, beginning with the Shaping Chicago's Future conference in 1988. From 1988 to 1992, in a series of Shaping America's Future forums and PBS video conferences, he brought together scores of national and world leaders including Al Shanker; Peter Senge; Mary Futrell; Linda Darling-Hammond;

Ed Zigler; and CEO's of GM, Ford, and other corporations to determine how best to bring quality concepts and those of "learning organizations" to bear in educational systems.

The HOPE Foundation provides professional development for thousands of educational leaders annually throughout North America and other parts of the world, including South Africa. HOPE also provides long-term support for school improvement through leadership academies and intensive onsite school change efforts, leading to dramatic increases in student achievement in diverse settings.

A former "high risk" youth, Blankstein began his career in education as a music teacher and has worked within youth-serving organizations for 20 years, including the March of Dimes, Phi Delta Kappa, and the National Educational Service (NES), which he founded in 1987 and directed for 12 years.

He coauthored with Rick DuFour the Reaching Today's Youth curriculum, now provided as a course in 16 states, and has contributed writing to *Educational Leadership, The School Administrator, Executive Educator, High School Magazine, Reaching Today's Youth,* and *EQ + IQ = Best Leadership Practices for Caring and Successful Schools.* Alan has provided keynote presentations and workshops for virtually every major educational organization. He is author of the best-selling book *Failure Is Not an Option™: Six Principles That Guide Student Achievement in High-Performing Schools,* which has been awarded "Book of the Year" by the National Staff Development Council and nominated for three other national and international awards.

Blankstein is on the Harvard International Principals Center's advisory board, has served as a board member for the Federation of Families for Children's Mental Health, is a cochair of Indiana University's Neal Marshall Black Culture Center's Community Network, and is advisor to the Faculty and Staff for Student Excellence mentoring program. He is also an advisory board member for the Forum on Race, Equity, and Human Understanding with the Monroe County Schools in Indiana, and has served on the Board of Trustees for the Jewish Child Care Agency (JCCA), at which he was once a youth-in-residence.

Robert W. Cole is Proprietor and Founder of Edu-Data, a firm specializing in writing, research, and publication services. He was a member of the staff of *Phi Delta Kappan* magazine for 14 years:

Assistant Editor from 1974 to 1976, Managing Editor from 1976 to 1980, and Editor-in-Chief from 1981 to 1988. During his tenure as Editor-in-Chief, the *Kappan* earned more than 40 Distinguished Achievement Awards from the Association of Educational Publishers, three of them for his editorials.

Since leaving the *Kappan,* Cole has served as founding Vice President of the Schlechty Center for Leadership in School Reform (CLSR) (1990–1994). At CLSR, he managed district- and community-wide school reform efforts and led the team that created the Kentucky Superintendents' Leadership Institute. He formed the Bluegrass Leadership Network, in which superintendents worked together to use current leadership concepts to solve reform-oriented management and leadership problems.

As senior consultant to the National Reading Styles Institute (1994–2005), Cole served as editor and lead writer of the Power Reading Program. He and a team of writers and illustrators created a series of hundreds of graded short stories, short novels, and comic books from primer through Grade 10. Those stories were then recorded by Cole and Dr. Marie Carbo; they are being used by schools all across the United States to teach struggling readers.

Cole has served as a book development editor for the Association for Supervision and Curriculum Development (ASCD), for Corwin Press, and for Writer's Edge Press. He has been president of the Educational Press Association of America and member of the EdPress Board of Directors. He has presented workshops, master classes, and lectures at universities nationwide, including Harvard University, Stanford University, Indiana University, Xavier University, Boise State University, and the University of Southern Maine. He has served as a special consultant to college and university deans in working with faculties on writing for professional publication. Recently, he began serving as Managing Editor and Senior Associate with the Center for Empowered Leadership.

ABOUT THE CONTRIBUTORS

Chuck Bonner has worked in the field of public education for 21 years. He has been a teacher at all grade levels in public education and has also worked as a K–12 department chair in school counseling. He is currently entering his sixth year as Assistant Principal at Great Valley High School in Malvern, Pennsylvania. Bonner has been working to develop awareness in equity and cultural competence in his current school district. He has also been involved in working with the high school's alternative education program. He received a BS from Temple University, an MS from Villanova University, and a PhD from Drexel University.

Terrence (Terry) E. Deal is a former teacher, principal, cop, and administrator who received his PhD in educational administration and sociology from Stanford University. He teaches courses in organizations and leadership and has previously taught at Stanford, Harvard, and Vanderbilt Universities, and the University of Southern California. Deal specializes in the study of organizations. He consults to a wide variety of organizations such as businesses, hospitals, banks, schools, colleges, religious orders, and military organizations in the United States and abroad.

Dr. Deal is included on a list of the world's leading management thinkers in the 2003 book *What's the Big Idea? Creating and Capitalizing on the Best New Management Thinking,* by Thomas H. Davenport, Laurence Prusak, and H. James Wilson. He was also ranked among "79 top management thinkers" in the 1998 book *The Guru Guide: the Best Ideas of the Top Management Thinkers,* by Joseph H. Boyett and Jimmie T. Boyett.

Dr. Deal has written 30 books and more than 100 articles and book chapters concerning organizations, leadership, change, culture, and symbolism and spirit. Many of these have been translated into languages such as Japanese, Korean, Chinese, Farsi, Dutch, French, Norwegian, Portuguese, German, Italian, and Spanish.

Bea Mah Holland, an executive coach and consultant for education, business, and health care, is committed to the learning and capacity building of people and their organizations. She combines her in-depth understanding of organizations with an invitation to individual reflection and action grounded in approaches such as appreciative inquiry, systems thinking, organizational learning, and positive psychology.

Action-oriented and focused on nurturing strengths, Dr. Holland's educational roles have included Director of Leadership and Senior Lecturer, MIT Sloan School of Management; Editorial Board member, *Harvard Educational Review;* Founding Partner, Center for Empowered Leadership (CFEL), consultant working with Harry Levinson of Harvard University; and Assistant Professor, University of Calgary Faculty of Social Welfare Dr. Holland's recent clients have included Wheaton College (MA), University of Memphis College of Education, and Fitchburg and Lexington Public Schools (MA), in addition to several business and health care clients.

She has also served as President of Pegasus Communications; Organizational Consultant and Leadership Program Manager at Digital Equipment Corporation; Coordinator of Executive Development, Massachusetts Department of Personnel Administration; and as a social worker and supervisor for Edmonton (Alberta) Social Services and Glenrose Hospital. Dr. Holland's thesis at Harvard University focused on the learning at the MIT Sloan School Senior Executives Program. For leisure, she enjoys traveling with her husband and two adult daughters.

Dawna Markova is internationally known for her groundbreaking work in helping people learn with passion and live on purpose. She is the CEO of Professional Thinking Partners, a group of consultants whose expertise lies in the expansion of human capacity, and Founder of www.smartwired.org, which is designed to recognize, develop, and utilize intellectual capital. Her books include *I Will Not Die an Unlived Life, The SMART Parenting Revolution, The Art of the Possible, The Open Mind, No Enemies Within, An Unused Intelligence, How Your Child Is Smart,* and *Learning Unlimited.* As one of the editors of the *Random Acts of Kindness* series, Dr. Markova helped launch a national movement to help counter America's crisis of violence. A former board member of the Visions for a Better World Foundation, she is very active in making the world a better place.

Christa Metzger is currently Professor Emeritus in the Department of Educational Leadership and Policy Studies at California State University, Northridge. She came to the university in 1996 from a successful career as teacher, principal, and district superintendent in California, Arizona, Florida, and Germany. Christa has a doctorate in educational administration from Arizona State University and has been actively involved in her profession. She has held leadership positions on many state, regional, and national boards, as well as in community and professional organizations. During the past 10 years, her active life has turned inward and has become more reflective. She has taught meditation in her church and has been writing to connect her love for her profession and her interest in spirituality. Her most recent book is entitled *Balancing Leadership and Personal Growth—The School Administrator's Guide* (2006, Corwin Press). She and her husband of 37 years just moved to their retirement home in a peaceful environment along the Neuse River on the Inner Banks of North Carolina. She plans to continue teaching online courses for the university from there.

Eric Schaps is Founder and President of the nonprofit Developmental Studies Center (DSC) in Oakland, California. Established in 1980, DSC specializes in designing educational programs and evaluating their effects on children's academic, ethical, social, and emotional development. Dr. Schaps is the author of three books and 75 book chapters and articles on educational policy and practice, school change, character education, preventing problem behaviors, and program evaluation. He serves on several boards including the education advisory board of the Boys & Girls Clubs of America. He received his PhD in social psychology from Northwestern University, where he also did his undergraduate work. He is married and has three children.

Claire Sheff Kohn currently is Superintendent of the Masconomet Regional School District in Massachusetts. She is the former superintendent of the Princeton Regional Schools in New Jersey and prior to that was superintendent in Lawrence Township, New Jersey, and in Hull, Massachusetts. She has served as a training consultant to districts and professional organizations on matters of leadership and strategic planning. She also mentors prospective and newly appointed superintendents. Dr. Kohn's earlier professional experiences include serving as an assistant superintendent, high school assistant principal, high school guidance counselor, and teacher of English. She earned her degrees from Stonehill College, Boston College, and the University of Massachusetts at Amherst.

Stephen L. Sokolow, a former superintendent of schools, is currently coauthoring a series of books on the spiritual principles of leadership. He is also a founding partner and Executive Director of the Center for Empowered Leadership (www.cfel.org). In 1986, Dr. Sokolow was selected by the *Executive Educator,* a publication of the National School Boards Association, as one of the top 100 small-district school executives in North America He was honored for his leadership as a superintendent by the New Jersey Legislature in 1987 and was profiled by *The School Administrator* for his "out-of-the-box thinking" in January of 1999. His feature article on "Enlightened Leadership" was published in September 2002 in *The School Administrator,* a national publication of the American Association of School Administrators, as was his November 2005 article on "Nourishing Our Spirit as Leaders." In 2006, he coauthored *The Spiritual Dimension of Leadership* (Corwin Press) with Dr. Paul Houston. Dr. Sokolow is a child-centered educator committed to empowering enlightened leadership in both the public and private sectors, but especially in the field of education.

Scott Thompson, who started his career as a high school English teacher, is author of *Leading From the Eye of the Storm: Spirituality and Public School Improvement.* He is Assistant Executive Director of the Panasonic Foundation, a corporate philanthropic organization that is wholly devoted to the improvement of public education in the United States, and Editor of *Strategies,* an issues series from the Panasonic Foundation in cooperation with the American Association of School Administrators and the University Council of Educational Administration. Before joining the staff of the Panasonic Foundation, Thompson was Director of Dissemination and Project Development at the Institute for Responsive Education and Editor of *New Schools, New Communities.* He lives with his wife, daughter, cat, and hermit crab in Glen Rock, New Jersey.

INTRODUCTION

ROBERT W. COLE

H ere we are at the very core of this project. It only makes sense, in an eight-part series on *The Soul of Educational Leadership,* that a volume titled *Spirituality in Educational Leadership* is smack in the middle. After all, the overall title signals that, as Paul Houston points out, "the work we do is really more of a calling and a mission than it is a job." Cornel West described it as "soul craft," and soul craft for educational leaders—preparing young people for life—includes both the most elevating rewards and the most soul-trying sacrifices.

In his opening chapter, Houston refers to spirituality as "the energy that connects us to each other and to our deepest selves." It is a central tenet of this series that educational leadership necessarily engages—and requires—the commitment of the deepest self of the leader who would hope to prevail. Take Standard 5 of the ISLLC *Standards for School Leaders*, for instance: "A school administrator is an educational leader who promotes the success of all students by acting with integrity, fairness, and in an ethical manner." A sound moral core is a prerequisite for the work of soul craft—for the role of leader in the educational arena. You will find, in this volume, that we address the issues of the search for meaning, core values, connectedness, trust of self and others, capacity building, moral and ethical development, making tough decisions, personal growth, and the whole delicate balancing act that is the art of leadership.

Early in 2007, Volume 1, *Engaging Every Learner,* signaled that every student matters deeply, to all of us in school and in our society. Alan Blankstein—editor of this series, together with Paul Houston and myself—sounded the theme that guides this entire series: "Saving young people from failure in school is equivalent to saving their lives!" We know how to do what needs doing, and in every volume we are enlisting the thinking of those who have led the way.

In Volume 2, *Out-of-the-Box Leadership,* Houston observed that schools have been making incremental progress in an exponential environment. "Deteriorating social conditions surrounding families and children," he wrote, "have confronted us with all sorts of new challenges." He called for transformative leadership, which can come only by thinking differently about our problems. Providing educators and educational leaders with such assistance is one over-arching purpose of this series.

How do we meet the difficult (some say impossible) challenge of holding onto—and improving upon—valuable work once it has begun? Volume 3, *Sustaining Learning Communities,* looked beyond inclusiveness and transformation to how best to work together to create learning communities that support enduring change. Andy Hargreaves, Thomas More Brennan Chair in Education at Boston College's Lynch School of Education, highlighted the need for educational leaders to be much more than managers or instructional leaders—"to be leaders of their students, their fellow professionals, their wider communities—and indeed of their societies as a whole in collective pursuit of a greater social good as professionals, community workers, and citizens."

That vision of leadership writ large continues in this, the fourth volume of *The Soul of Educational Leadership.* Appropriately, as lead editor of this volume, Houston begins by asking "What's Spirituality Got to Do With It?" His answer is this: "As I talked with leaders across the country, I found a longing for meaning and comfort. These jobs of ours as educational leaders are difficult and draining. They sap our physical and moral energy. We have to find ways of replenishing the supply." The demands of leadership leave us with two choices: "change our careers or connect to the power that we share with others and with the divine. That is why having a spiritual sense of what we do is so important."

"Many of the core values and principles that have guided and sustained us as leaders have underlying spiritual roots," write Stephen

Sokolow and Paul Houston in the chapter titled "The Spiritual Dimension of Leadership." (A former superintendent of schools, Sokolow is founding partner and executive director of the Center for Empowered Leadership.) They make the key distinction that "spiritual" is not used in a religious sense here, but rather as a way of describing ways of thinking, being, and doing that are life-sustaining and life-enhancing both for individuals and organizations. Enlightened leadership creates the means to bring more wisdom to the world and "to shape a better future for our organizations and the children we serve."

Unfortunately, "there are many forces that are trying to convince us more of our separation than of our connection," writes Dawna Markova in her chapter, "Spiritual Courage: Leading From the Inside Out." Markova—a psychotherapist, a researcher, and a consultant to leaders of organizations from education to health care to corporations—has heard educational leaders longing to find coherence and meaning amid chaos, and she counsels, "Begin to trust your own inner resources to guide you." The old stories and mythologies and certainties that we have clung to for generations no longer work, she tells us; we need "to create new stories that will unify us." To connect ourselves with the imaginative and creative process that can carry us forward, "we must relearn to become comfortable with the inner aspect of ourselves that feels lost." In so doing, "We may find that we are held and guided by hidden hands."

All living systems are replete with solutions, says Bea Mah Holland, a one-time director of leadership for the MIT Sloan School of Management. In her chapter, "Appreciative Inquiry: A Strategy for Reshaping Education That Builds on Strengths and Hopes," she uses her experience as a strength-based coach and consultant who is committed to individual and organizational learning and capacity building. Appreciative Inquiry is based in spirit because it taps into the inner aspect of a person's highest consciousness. The AI process "helps people find meaning as they use their highest strengths in service to something larger than themselves"—and thus the larger group's aspirations can emerge from the core of every individual member.

Eric Schaps founded the Developmental Studies Center (DSC) in 1980 to specialize in designing and evaluating educational programs that promote children's social, ethical, and academic development. In his chapter, "Community in School: The Heart of the Matter," he shows how leaders' knowledge of students and their experience of schooling is fundamental to effective leadership. Ensuring that students' experience of school is positive is a moral as well as a pragmatic imperative, he emphasizes. Students are entrusted to their school's care, and so educational leaders are morally obliged to see that young people are safe and supported.

A school superintendent for 19 years (currently in the Masconomet School District in Massachusetts), Claire Sheff-Kohn writes, "I make decisions that affect people's lives and livelihoods. In making those decisions, I struggle to do my best to determine what's right and to act accordingly. But how do I know what's right?" In "The Stories of Practicing Superintendents: The Struggle to Make the Right Decisions," she interviewed 10 colleagues about their basic values, where those values came from, and how they guide superintendents in making tough decisions.

How do leaders engage in their own personal growth and develop their spirituality—not only on their own time, but in the place where they work, on the job, during the workday? A former superintendent and faculty member at California State University, Christa Metzger polled educational administrators and business executives in "Personal Growth in the Workplace: Spiritual Practices You Can Use." Her findings, she reported, "provide hope that leaders are coming to be aware of the importance of developing their own inner and spiritual dimensions—and that they're finding that it's possible to do this as part of everyday life, even at work."

"A spiritually oriented leader seeks more than just quantitative change, such as higher scores on standardized tests," writes Chuck Bonner, an assistant principal at Great Valley High School in Malvern, Pennsylvania, in his chapter, "Spiritually Oriented Leadership in a Secular Age." Unfortunately, "bottom-line thinking has come to pervade education." At the school-building level, he reminds us that "all the policies and laws and tests happen to real people—people I know. They happen to people who trust me with their children." Only the cultivation of spiritually oriented leaders can bring about the changes that are needed in public education. But for such changes to occur—and Bonner believes that they *must* occur—the first, and most important, changes need to take place within ourselves.

The "inner world" of individual leaders is rooted in "heart and consciousness and spirituality," writes Scott Thompson in "Spiritual Leadership—the Invisible Revolution." Thompson, who began his career as a high school English teacher, is assistant executive director of the Panasonic Foundation. He advocates "bringing the whole self, including spiritual resources, to bear on the tangible problems that leaders must face in the complicated world of schools and districts." A "revolutionizing of human consciousness" is needed to accomplish the "revolutionary changes" that are now needed in our educational system," he concludes, affirming Margaret Wheatley's dictum that "leadership today is spiritual."

"Leadership is a balancing act," Terrence Deal notes in the concluding chapter, "Leadership on a Teeter-Totter: Balancing Rationality and Spirituality." The Irving R. Melbo Professor at the University of Southern California's Rossier School, Deal adds, "An overly logical organization lacks vigor; an overly zealous, spirit-driven enterprise often lacks rigor. . . . Either structural or spiritual disequilibrium damages performance." The bad news, as he sees it, is this:

> For some time, schools have been overmanaged and under-led. Management is on the control-and-consequences end of the teeter-totter. Leadership, focusing on passion and purpose, is on the opposite end. The imbalance has taken its toll on the spiritual underbelly of education. To regain the proper and necessary equilibrium between systems and soul, superintendents and principals at the local level need to focus less on the mechanics of instruction and more on the deeper meaning of teaching and learning.

Terry Deal points out that there is no need to sacrifice an attention to standards and accountability, but there is a need—an urgent one—to *balance* them with passion and purpose. "The pressing issue today is not improving test scores," Deal writes—it is "reviving the spirit of education, and restoring hope and faith in the deeper value that schools offer to the lives of young people." He concludes, "If we don't do something now to correct the imbalance in our schools, we will reap some very costly consequences in the near future. It is a terrible price that our nation cannot afford to pay."

Helping you tend to the spiritual side of your role as an educational leader is one of the guiding purposes of *The Soul of Educational Leadership*. We sincerely hope that you find some measure of nurturance and strength that assists you within these pages.

CHAPTER ONE

WHAT'S SPIRITUALITY GOT TO DO WITH IT?

PAUL D. HOUSTON

Several years ago, I started injecting the issue of spirituality into my speeches to our members. I also started writing about spirituality in my articles. Since I head an organization—the American Association of School Administrators (AASA)—made up of public school administrators, and since we are living in a time when people are very sensitive to issues that concern religion, I did this with some trepidation. After all, we are very concerned in our business about maintaining the separation of church and state. Besides, some might wonder what the issue of spirit has to do with educational leadership. After all, leadership is about getting things done, right? Spirituality strikes many as a little "soft" and out of place in the rough-and-tumble world of school leadership.

First, the separation issue is important. It is clear to me that it is inappropriate for the government to use its power and resources to establish religion. However, I believe that religions are specific to particular faiths and ways of believing, whereas spirituality is generic and transcends religion. To better explain my thinking about this knotty issue, let me suggest the metaphor of pipes. There are all kinds of pipes—large, small, plastic, copper, round, oblong, and so forth. These pipes are like religions. They come in all forms. They are shaped by the dogma and specific belief system of that particular flavor of belief. You choose the pipe that best suits your needs.

I am, for instance, by tradition and family background a Methodist. My father was a Methodist minister, so I had little choice. As I got older, I stayed with the tradition—so I am a Bible-thumping, hymn-singing Methodist from the hills of West Virginia and proud of it. That, however, is merely the *form* of my belief system. It's the *substance* that counts; it is what flows through the pipes that is important. And what flows through the pipes is essentially the same whether you are a Buddhist or a Jew or a Moslem or a Methodist. Religion gives us a rubric for working with the deity—and spirituality is the energy that connects us to the deity. It is also the energy that connects us to each other and to our deepest selves.

These jobs of ours as educational leaders are difficult and draining. They sap our physical and moral energy. We have to find ways of replenishing the supply.

Second, as I talked with leaders all across the country, I found a longing for meaning and comfort. These jobs of ours as educational leaders are difficult and draining. They sap our physical and moral energy. We have to find ways of replenishing the supply. One way we do that is by going inside and finding that part of ourselves that is more than just flesh and bones. I have pointed out that the work we do is really more of a calling and a mission than it is a job—what Cornel West once described as "soul craft." It is difficult to reconcile the work of leaders as strictly management when so much of it deals with people's aspirations and dreams—when so much of it affirms or denies people's very essence. When you affect people's lives, you best be aware of the spiritual nature of what you are doing—because at the core of our humanity is that golden cord of connection to the infinite. All leaders must be attuned to the third dimension beyond thinking and doing—to what it is to "be" a human in touch with the divine. But educational leaders, because of their responsibility for the future through touching the lives of children, have an even greater obligation.

For this reason alone, I began talking about the spiritual nature of our work. Then a funny thing happened on the way to the controversy I anticipated. Rather than creating protest, that was the one part of what I was saying that prompted the most follow-up and support! It was clear that there is a hunger in our midst for finding our deeper purpose and for conducting our work in a more enlightened manner.

So I suggested to our magazine editor at AASA that we publish an edition on the issue of spirituality and leadership. It became one of the most popular editions we had ever published. People gobbled up the extra copies; today you can't even find one. At the same time, my friend Steve Sokolow and I had been having rather deep conversations about spirituality and leadership; those talks led us to found the Center for Empowered Leadership and to publish *The Spiritual Dimension of Leadership* (Corwin, 2006). All of this also led me to suggest this topic to Corwin as a part of this series of books on *The Soul of Educational Leadership.* The writers herein do not necessarily always agree with each other, but as you read this volume you will be treated to a journey of discovery, as thoughtful people grapple with what to say on the subject of spirituality and leadership. What they *do* agree on is that it is an important topic and one worth every leader's concern and deep engagement.

Deepak Chopra (2002) has pointed out that leaders are the symbolic soul of the groups they lead and that great leaders respond from the higher levels of spirit. In the piece he wrote for *School Administrator,* Chopra suggested that in our chaotic environment, it is the leader who thrives on the chaos because that person understands the underlying spiritual order. Leaders must make the choice to "step out of the darkness," he said, and only one who can find wisdom in the midst of chaos will be remembered as a leader.

But leadership does not exist only at the 30,000-foot level. Leaders influence what happens on the ground in organizations. One of the paradoxes of true spiritual leaders is that they are lofty, but lowly at the same time. They rise above the fray, but they also must be willing to get their hands dirty. Having a core of spiritual ballast allows leaders to make certain that as they are getting their hands dirty, they are not sullying their organizations or their core principles. It also allows them to bind up the tattered parts of the organization and create healing. But while they are doing that, they are also tying together the infinite and the sublime.

Ellen Langer (1989) has written eloquently about the need for leaders to have a sense of "mindfulness" as they go about their work. Mindfulness, which she believes is the essence of leadership, allows a leader to be fully engaged at all times. Langer has cited research by her and her colleagues demonstrating that mindfulness creates an attraction to others and for others, thus creating a compact between leader and led that allows leadership to blossom fully. Leaders must be constantly aware—not simply staying on guard but staying in the game—to allow them to connect in all ways to those in need.

I believe—and I am not alone in so believing—that we all need a sacred narrative to give us a sense of larger purpose. Only by connecting to our purpose do we come to understand and to accept the personal sacrifices we must make every day. Leadership is a life of giving. Having a connection to spirituality allows the leader to refill the well and to progress toward an uncertain future.

Another major role for the leader is to create a sense of community. Educators and politicians are fond of reminding the public that it takes a village to raise a child. The irony of this African proverb is that in our modern, frantic, disconnected existence, we don't really have the sense of village any longer. Leaders must provide guidance in helping to foster that sense of village by creating a sense of community. The leader is the person who has been designated as the first member of any community. It is his or her responsibility to open doors to new possibilities—among them, a stronger sense of connectedness to one another.

I have tried to remind school leaders that their job is to turn lights on, not off. They must create the environment and possibility of success. They must do that through trust and forgiveness.

I have tried to remind school leaders that their job is to turn lights on, not off. They must create the environment and possibility of success. They must do that through trust and forgiveness. No leader has ever successfully delegated a task to another without being able to feel (and to engender) a sense of trust. The leader must believe that the one who has been given the responsibility can do it, and then the leader must be able to forgive that person for not doing it the way the leader would have done the same task. Only through these things can community be created. Leadership isn't shouldering the burden of being the Lone Ranger—the sole superhero who steps to in to ward off disaster. True leadership is carried out through others.

As a young man, I was fascinated by John F. Kennedy. He was a president who seemed young and vital, witty and articulate. But what I remember about him most clearly is that he constantly referred to the leadership quality of having "grace under pressure." Again, my religious tradition had much to say about grace. I suspect that President Kennedy saw grace as a sense of elegance and smoothness and decency. From the religious tradition, grace also is a generosity of spirit, a prayer of thanksgiving, and the infinite love of God toward humankind. Most simply, it is a core ingredient of good leadership. One is tempted to point out that amazing leaders show amazing grace. Solid leaders are both effective—they make a difference in their organization—and affective—they make a difference in the lives of those around them.

I need not remind anyone working in education today that the work is difficult. It can be grimy and soul-wearying. If it were easy, someone else would be doing it. Leadership in today's context seems Sisyphean—you just have to keep rolling that rock up the hill, knowing all the time that someone will come along and try to roll it back down. Conducting yourself in such a difficult and challenging context creates a sense of trying your soul. I believe that in this context we have only two choices: change our careers or connect to the power that we share with others and with the divine. That is why having a spiritual sense of what we do is so important.

In the next chapter, my friend and coconspirator Steve Sokolow takes the lead in summarizing some of the work he and I are doing together on the issue of enlightened leaders. Steve and I are working on a series of books on the subject and are searching for ways of helping leaders find that special place we all have that will allow them to have the strength to do the work that needs to be done. We believe that managers do things right and leaders do the right things—but *enlightened and empowered* leaders do the right things in the right way and for the right reasons. Steve and I believe that each of us does the work we do because it is at the core of who we are. That is both the gift and the curse of educational leaders. Our work has such meaning, yet it is hard to separate it from our essence. Before you go somewhere, you not only need to know *where* you are going, but also *who* you are on the journey.

I have pointed out that our role as leaders bears a much closer connection to that of ministers than it does to CEOs. Our authority comes not from our position, but from the moral authority we are entrusted to carry as we build a future through the children of our community. We get our work done, not through mandate and fiat, but by gathering folks together and persuading them to do what is right. To carry out this task requires a higher connection than that of the direct line to the state department of education or the president of the school board.

Thus we begin our journey through very lightly explored territory. It is my hope that as you read through this book, you will come back to the core essence of what I have come to believe: *spiritual leaders lead from within.* They must know themselves and have a sense of purpose and connection to the infinite. But they live in this world as well, and the impact of what they do affects others. Their ultimate goal must be to have an effect that is greater than one person's alone—and to remember that on this earth, God's work must truly be our own.

REFERENCES

Chopra, D. (2002, September). The soul of leadership. *School Administrator, 59,* 8.

Langer, E. (1989). *Mindfulness.* Reading, MA: Addison-Wesley.

CHAPTER TWO

THE SPIRITUAL DIMENSION OF LEADERSHIP

STEPHEN L. SOKOLOW AND PAUL D. HOUSTON

P aul Houston and I started out as professional colleagues—superintendents in school districts not far from each other. We came to know each other well as we attended a series of summer programs for superintendents at Harvard University. As we talked about our challenges, our frustrations, and our victories, we found that most of the time we weren't talking about education or even leadership per se—we were talking about our spiritual values and the underlying connections between who we were at the deepest level and what we did on a day-to-day basis. These discussions started us on a joint expedition of the soul that has led to a 20-year conversation about

In large measure, this chapter is an abridged version of *The Spiritual Dimension of Leadership: 8 Key Principles to Leading More Effectively* (Corwin Press, 2006), by Dr. Paul D. Houston, executive director of the American Association of School Administrators, and Dr. Stephen L. Sokolow, executive director of the Center for Empowered Leadership. In our book, we describe 8 key principles from an array of 42 spiritual principles of leadership we have identified. The full array is available at www.cfel.org.

what it truly means to be a human being and the implications of that awareness for our work as educational leaders.

We have come to realize that many of the core values and principles that have guided and sustained us as leaders have underlying spiritual roots.

We have come to realize that many of the core values and principles that have guided and sustained us as leaders have underlying spiritual roots. We selected eight of these principles to focus on in this chapter because they represent various aspects of the energy of mind, body, and spirit—or what we think of as the energy of head, hand, and heart. We use the word *spiritual* not in a religious sense per se, but rather to describe ways of thinking, being, and doing that are life-sustaining and life-enhancing both for individuals and organizations. As with anything in the spiritual realm, our respective understandings of these principles are works in progress—as are all human beings. These principles are not something you can check off on your "to do" list. They are habits of mind and soul that can act as guideposts for the perilous and wonderful journey we call the spiritual dimension of leadership.

KEY ONE: THE PRINCIPLE OF INTENTION

Intention is a framework for the creation of ultimate reality. It's the building plan for reality. Before you can have a plan, you've got to have an intention—the thought of what you want to see happen, or where you want to go, or what your ultimate goal is. From that beginning, you can start developing plans.

Sending your intention out into the Universe creates energy. It creates an energy cycle that is largely outside of your control once you send it out. So you're not just acting from your own center; you're also enlisting the aid of a lot of other seen and unseen powers outside of you. You're stirring the pot of energy that the Universe makes available when you create a sense of what you want to do and why you want to do it.

You can think of an intention as the ripples a stone makes skipping along the surface of a pond. Each time it touches the pond, the stone generates a series of ever-expanding concentric circles; the sets of circles intersect and overlap at some point. The pattern created by an intention is similar to the surface of the pond after the stone passes by, but because the medium is life and not water, the reverberations travel like light and do not lose strength as they contribute to the fabric of life.

Most leaders do not have a strong enough appreciation of the power of intention as a force for shaping reality. People do or want to do so many things that it's not always clear what their intentions are. So it's very important for leaders to have clear in their own mind what their intentions are—not only what they would like to see happen in a particular set of circumstances or in a particular dynamic, but also what motivation lies one step beneath the goal itself. Besides knowing what your goals are in any given set of circumstances, you should also, to the extent that it is possible, ask yourself about your primary motivation. This is a personal process between you and your inner or higher self—and, perhaps ultimately, the divine. That internal dialogue about what you want to do and why you want to do it ignites the spark that is emitted into the Universe as an energy field.

For example, you could have a goal of losing weight, but your underlying intention is to be healthy. *The intention is more fundamental than the goal.* The intention can even create a set of goals. The goals themselves are not the intention; the intention is underneath the goal and explains *why*. Why would *you* want to be healthy (beyond the fact that everyone does)? Your intention to be healthy may tie into your need to have sufficient energy to make a more positive contribution to the world or to meet your professional responsibilities. So your intention ties into a more fundamental set of reasons about why you want to do something.

As a leader, the intentions that carry the most force are those that will benefit people other than yourself. But that doesn't mean that your intentions can't also benefit you! You can benefit from being healthy, but by being healthy you are also in a better position to serve others. Intention is part of the dance of attunement between you and the Universe—a term that we use in the sense of a higher spiritual power. When you're attuned, everyone benefits. When you're out of attunement, no one benefits. And that's a good reason for wanting to be attuned with the Universe, because whatever happens for the Universe happens for you, too. There's a mutual interplay between you and the Universe. When your intentions are strictly selfish, the Universe is unlikely to assist you; consequently, the Universe won't benefit either. So you have to be thoughtful, with some sense of clarity, when you formulate your intentions.

We all affect eternity by our thought patterns, our words, and our deeds. They emit energy fields that contribute to the fabric that is woven into the unfolding pattern of life. Again, what we think, say, and do always has a crucial underlying element, which is our intention or intended purpose. Our intention can be expressed in countless ways, but the better we know ourselves the more aware we can be of our own true intentions. The more closely our intentions are aligned with our inner being and our life's purposes, the happier and more fulfilled we are—and the more effective we are as leaders.

The more closely our intentions are aligned with our inner being and our life's purposes, the happier and more fulfilled we are—and the more effective we are as leaders.

Intention also serves as a powerful force in attracting people, material resources, and other energies that can help us transform our intentions into reality. Enlightened leaders are aware of their intentions and naturally focus them on serving others rather than themselves.

You may want to remember that enlightened leaders

- Understand the power of intention
- Use the power of thought to help shape reality
- Use the power of prayer to manifest their intentions
- Use the spoken and written word to manifest their intentions
- Align their actions with their intentions
- Enlist spiritual and nonspiritual forces to manifest their intentions
- Use their insight and intuition to manifest their intentions
- Use attention to manifest their intentions
- Focus their energy to manifest their intentions
- Use the power of will to manifest their intentions

KEY TWO: THE PRINCIPLE OF ATTENTION

How many times have your teachers said something like, "Pay attention" or "Are you paying attention?" In the military, people really get serious about it and say, "Atten-hut! Eyes forward, stand erect, stand still, and listen up!" Educators know that attention is a key component of learning, but it's much more than that.

Attention is a way of focusing energy—your energy: mental, physical, and emotional—as well as the mental, physical, and emotional energy of others. If you believe in higher realms of existence, attention is also a way of focusing spiritual energy. The central tenet of this principle is the marvelous adage: *Where attention goes, energy flows.* If you want something to thrive and grow, pay attention to it. On the other hand, if you want something to wither and diminish, don't pay attention to it; intentionally ignore it.

As with most things, there are exceptions, but as a general rule of thumb, this perspective serves us well.

One of the most important choices you make as a leader is to decide what you want to pay attention to. In fact, what *you* want to pay attention to may often not be the same as what everybody else wants you to pay attention to.

- You pay attention by what you think about.
- You pay attention by what you talk about and what you ask about.
- You pay attention by what you write about and what you look at.
- You pay attention by what you do.

When leaders pay attention to a person, a situation, or an issue, others start to pay attention to the same things, whether you want them to or not. Therefore, you need to be mindful about what you pay attention to. Leaders are attention magnets.

Try this experiment. The next time you're in a group setting, look to the left and raise your eyebrow—watch how others in the group follow your gaze. They'll want to

- See what you see,
- Hear what you hear, and
- Do what you do.

The whole notion of being a role model flows from the *principle of attention.* If no one paid attention to you, none of what you are modeling would make a difference. It wouldn't be emulated. This principle is more complex than it seems because attention is both conscious and unconscious. For an example of the power of unconscious attention, just look at the way media marketers use subliminal advertising. In other words, even when people are not aware that they are paying attention, the unconscious mind is absorbing vast quantities of information from what is perceived subliminally.

There is a level of attention that seems to flow naturally from observing the leader, but there's also another form of attention leaders create by requiring people to work on something, especially if there are penalties and rewards involved. For example, is anybody paying attention to the requirements of the president's No Child Left Behind (NCLB) initiative in public education? Most definitely, largely due to the penalties and rewards associated with it.

The principle of attention can be used for good or for ill, which brings us back to the Principle of Intention that we briefly described earlier. We believe that when your attention is aligned with the higher aspects of your being and with your higher purpose, the Universe (again, a term we use to betoken a higher spiritual power) will try to assist you and support you in many ways, both seen and unseen. Moreover, increasing the attention you give to your intentions increases the likelihood they will actually become a reality.

Enlightened leaders have insights that guide them in deciding where best to turn their attention. They tend to pay attention to the right things and do so for the right reasons.

We all have the same 24 hours to fill each day. How do we choose to spend that time? We continually make choices about the amount of time we will spend thinking, the amount of time we will spend doing, and the amount of time we will spend just being, as well as what we will choose to focus on. Some people or tasks demand our attention while other aspects of our attention are like discretionary income, to be spent as we wish.

Enlightened leaders have insights that guide them in deciding where best to turn their attention They tend to pay attention to the right things and do so for the right reasons. Our attention is powerful because it serves as a magnet that attracts others and helps us collectively align our energies. What we attend to shapes what we create, and what we create helps shape our reality.

You may want to remember that enlightened leaders

- Understand the key role attention plays in leadership
- Focus their attention through thought
- Focus their attention through action
- Focus their attention through being
- Know how to use their time effectively
- Focus power and energy on important issues and initiatives
- Know that attention is a magnet for enlisting others
- Pay attention to get attention paid
- Keep their focus
- Minimize distractions
- Use images, signs, and symbols to focus attention and create common purpose

KEY THREE: THE PRINCIPLE OF UNIQUE GIFTS AND TALENTS

First it was fingerprints, then voiceprints and retinal scans, and now DNA that show each human being is truly unique, a one-of-a-kind original. Yet that uniqueness is not just physical. Minds are unique, and so are spirits. But uniqueness extends even further—each person has unique gifts and talents as well.

Part of your task in life is to figure out what your unique gifts and talents are, how to cultivate them, and how to share them. So first you must identify your gifts and talents. Then, once you have a sense of what they are, you need to cultivate and develop them. Finally, you need to share them. As leaders, you are challenged not only to live and model that process but also to facilitate it in others. As leaders in the field of education, you have the opportunity to facilitate the process of identifying, cultivating, and sharing gifts, both for the people with whom you work and for the children you serve. When you do this, it is empowering for all whose lives are touched.

Middle schools offer a variety of exploratory programs—the theory being that you have to put kids through a lot of different experiences so they can explore many things to see where they might have talents or interests. As people grow up, however, they lose sight of the idea that life should be a constant exploration. If you are not willing to try something different, then you're never going to find out what your gifts are.

The most interesting people we know are people who are constantly on a mission, a quest, to learn new things. What they're saying is, "I may discover other things I'm good at and interested in. I just don't know because I've never tried them." On the other hand, we know other people who don't want to try anything new because they're happy where they are—even if they're really stuck in a rut. They have found one or two things they are really good at or enjoy, and they just keep doing them.

One piece of advice we give to young leaders is never to try to polish the same side twice. If you're good at something, don't keep polishing it. Go polish something else because that way, ultimately, you end up being shiny all over. If you only polish one side, you will have a lot of dull sides left over that you haven't developed. It is a constant struggle to fight against your natural instincts to stay with what you know because you are comfortable doing the things you know you are good at. Most people are much more talented than they will ever know. You may have talents and gifts at a certain level that you never use; at another level, you probably have capacities that you never even tap.

It is important to focus on gifts and talents, both of which are plural. We presume that you have more than one gift and more than one talent and that discovering all your gifts and talents is a lifelong journey. At different times in your life—your teenage years, your early adulthood, midlife, or old age—different gifts and talents emerge or come to the fore. Understanding that, you can be alert to clues that you have a talent or a gift in a given area. Life offers opportunities to discover and cultivate the talents that you have, but the choice of whether or not to do so is yours. One of the keys to discovering your talents is openness to your environment, to what other people are mirroring for you, and to what they see as your gifts and talents.

Truly, each of us is blessed with unique gifts and talents. We are each a piece in a three-dimensional puzzle of life, striving to figure out where we fit. And just like a puzzle, life is incomplete without us. Each of us is important to the whole. Enlightened leaders help others see the contours of their lives so they can see how they can best contribute to the whole.

Enlightened leaders strive to help others identify their own gifts and talents and then cultivate them, helping them find their place in the puzzle. Some enlightened leaders may even see the gifts that others have before they themselves are aware of them. When we recognize our own unique gifts, we want to share them with the world. Enlightened leaders facilitate this process.

Enlightened leaders help others see the contours of their lives so they can see how they can best contribute to the whole.

We are continually given the opportunity to learn and to grow and to manifest the gifts that we have been given. We also can gain insight into our unique gifts and talents by reflecting on our life experiences and connecting with our divine spark, our higher or true self. Enlightened leaders are aware of this process and are ever alert to the opportunity to shine light on the potential in others.

It may be helpful to remember that enlightened leaders

- Have an awareness that everyone has unique gifts and talents
- Seek to discover and cultivate their own unique gifts and talents
- Help others to discover and cultivate their own unique gifts and talents
- Help others to share their unique gifts and talents
- Use partnership and interpersonal relationships to extend the unique gifts and talents of others
- Know that our uniqueness contributes to the evolving tapestry of life
- Know that events and synchronicities help us discover and cultivate our unique gifts and talents
- Know that the Universe, by which we mean a higher spiritual power, assists us in clarifying our life's purpose

---

KEY FOUR: THE PRINCIPLE OF GRATITUDE

There's an adage we are fond of: *Have an attitude of gratitude.* You can't be too grateful. Gratitude has a real, almost magical power. The key, however, is that it must be real. If it is insincere or pro forma, there is no magical ripple effect. Leaders get countless opportunities to show gratitude. Heaven knows they ought to be really grateful to the people they work with; for without them, leaders literally couldn't accomplish anything.

When you show gratitude for the help and support you receive, the impact multiplies—the good stuff just keeps coming. Gratitude creates plentitude. You end up with more, and when you are not grateful, you typically end up with less. Lacking gratitude, even those who have much may experience life as empty and sterile because they don't appreciate what they have. Gratitude is a magic word, the "Open Sesame!" of life. When you know how to be grateful and can express gratitude in appropriate terms, the rock rolls away, and the treasure is revealed.

Gratitude begets gratitude. Its expression attracts similar energy in others and in the Universe so that the very act of expressing gratitude sends out an energy field that not only comes back but also is magnified. Think of it as sprinkling Miracle-Gro in the garden of life. Gratitude has the effect of almost magically creating abundance; you sprinkle it out there and watch everything grow.

People tell little children that the magic words are "please" and "thank you." They are still magic words even when you grow up. Saying "thank you" is expressing gratitude. How many notes do you write to people expressing your gratitude? Do you appreciate how important those notes are to people? The words are important. You may *say* thank you, but if you take the next step and put the words in writing, they are even more powerful. You can use e-mail or print a letter off your computer, but the message will mean more if you write a note or letter by hand. Handwriting seems so much stronger than electronic communication because it is more personal. We save expressions of gratitude that we have received, and imagine that you might do so as well.

Think about something for which you are grateful: your current job, your family, your home, your education, your health, and so forth. Then trace the chain of events and people who played a role in bringing about whatever it is you are grateful about. How does this process work? First, you become aware that you are indeed grateful for something. Then you have the opportunity to express that gratitude

- To yourself;
- To the people to whom you are grateful;
- To wider audiences, actually sharing what it is you are grateful for and to whom; and
- To life, or to a higher spiritual power.

Think of all this as seeing with grateful eyes and expressing what you see with a grateful heart.

People often view gratitude in a range that is too narrow: as something that you feel when someone does something good for you—for example, being grateful for a favor or a gift. The attitude of gratitude, as we see it, is much broader than that. It's a way of looking at life that accepts and is grateful for whatever life brings you—good, bad, or ugly. An attitude of gratitude transcends the specific interchange that might be taking place; it is not simply, "I'm grateful for the gift or I'm grateful for the favor," but also "I'm grateful for the hurt, too; I'm grateful for the negative lesson that you brought me; I'm grateful for this difficult period that I am experiencing because it will help me learn or grow or be stronger." Having an attitude of gratitude is an approach to life that embraces whatever comes.

In life, new ideas and understandings arrive at different times and in different ways. The whole concept of having an attitude of gratitude is something that you can adopt and make a part of your worldview. An attitude of gratitude is one of the lenses that is available to you always, not just at specific times. Sometimes you need to remind yourself gently when the attitude is eluding you. When you are down or things aren't going well, gratitude may seem counterintuitive, but it is vitally needed. When you look at everything through grateful eyes, you will always see events, people, and experiences to be grateful for. To help you remember this, you might consider creating a small sign that says, "Have an attitude of gratitude."

It has been said that you cannot be too rich or too thin. That's certainly debatable, but we would argue that you cannot be too grateful. Enlightened leaders are grateful to the people around them and to life itself for the countless gifts they have been given. They have an "attitude of gratitude" and show it both internally and externally.

Enlightened leaders are grateful to the people around them and to life itself for the countless gifts they have been given. They have an "attitude of gratitude" and show it both internally and externally.

Gratitude is not just a feeling; it is a form of energy. Gratitude begets gratitude. The energy of gratitude has the power to attract and empower. We know that when we appreciate others, they are more likely to appreciate us. Similarly, when we appreciate the unique gifts of others, they are more likely to appreciate our unique gifts.

Gratitude and appreciation are among those special possessions that you can give away but still possess. Enlightened leaders abound with gratitude for the honor of serving others.

You may find it helpful to remember that enlightened leaders

- Have an attitude of gratitude
- Are mindful of life's blessings
- Show they are grateful for the help and support they receive
- Know the importance of being grateful for progress
- Know that progress is a measurement of life's blessings
- Are grateful for obstacles and adversaries
- Show gratitude for love received
- Show gratitude for love accepted
- Show gratitude for the opportunity to help others
- Show gratitude for their gifts and talents
- Know what it means to be grateful
- Know that gratitude is boundless
- Know that gratitude begets gratitude
- See gratitude as an important spiritual principle
- Are grateful for divine guidance

KEY FIVE: THE PRINCIPLE OF UNIQUE LIFE LESSONS

Roseanne Roseannadanna, a character made famous by the late Gilda Radner on the popular *Saturday Night Live* show, used to observe, "It just goes to show, it's always something. If it's not one thing, it's something else." You are always experiencing something and, whether you like it or not, that "something" seems to be designed to promote your growth as a human being. Every time you learn one life lesson, life seems to conjure up a new one in an unrelenting cycle. There simply is no safe haven from the vicissitudes of life.

Nonetheless, you get to decide how you look at whatever comes your way—you can choose to see it as a problem or as an opportunity. Almost any problem can be seen as an opportunity to grow and learn. That doesn't mean the problem isn't difficult or painful or frustrating or aggravating or costly. It just means that there's always a way to view or frame your experiences as opportunities for growth.

When we run into difficulties, we should ask ourselves, "Is there a lesson here? Is there some way I can learn and grow from this experience?" The potential lessons aren't always clear at first because they may be part of a larger pattern. But if they are important, they usually surface in a variety of places and circumstances. It may be helpful to examine recurring problems in your life to see if there is a discernable pattern that is calling you to change in some way.

In *Sacred Contracts,* best-selling author Caroline Myss (2001) says that people actually come to Earth with a contract that includes the lessons they want to learn, and that people are all working on their own unique life lessons. This is "Earth school," she asserts, and everyone has a curriculum designed to promote personal growth. Whether you agree with her perspective or not, it is a useful way of looking at the challenges and difficulties that confront you.

The more reflective you are, the more you will have some awareness that a lesson is unfolding. You can learn to view the experiences in your personal and professional lives—both those you consider positive and those that seem problematic—as potential lessons for your own benefit and growth.

One of the difficulties many people have when confronted with a problem is that they start stepping forward to meet it when often more progress may be made by stepping back. If you train yourself to pause and step back as a challenge confronts you, you'll have a chance to look at the bigger picture and to gain a full appreciation of what you are up against. We know we are most effective when we stop and look at the whole situation first, even though human nature and all our training is telling us to get out our problem-solving tools and dig in. If you move too quickly, you might be busily solving something that isn't really the problem—or at least isn't the right problem.

Sometimes solving the problem requires you to behave in a different way, in effect, to make a professional or personal change—a form of growth—in order to deal appropriately with whatever you encounter. Besides trying to use your skills to solve the problem, you can look through a different lens and ask yourself whether there might be a message from the Universe that you have an opportunity to grow. Unfortunately, people often externalize things, looking for solutions in the situation instead of asking themselves, "Is there something internal, within me, that needs to change?"

People tend to resist life's lessons instead of embracing them. When you embrace a problem, it is important to recognize that there may be a lesson operating as well. You are the participant, but you are also the observer in your own life. As you step back in the role of observer to gain perspective, think about what lessons may be unfolding for you.

Life can be seen as a series of unfolding lessons that enable us to grow and become our best selves. Embedded in the challenges and vicissitudes of life are opportunities for growth and self-expression. Enlightened leaders look at the events around them and the challenges they are confronting not only with an eye toward meeting those challenges, but also searching within themselves for the life lessons embedded in their experiences.

The Universe almost demands that we pay attention to that which can change our lives If we understand and appreciate the lesson, our reward is usually another lesson, for each lesson becomes a stairway to the next. If we ignore the important lessons that come to us, they often escalate and come at us again in a more difficult form.

Enlightened leaders not only contend with their own lessons, but also help others identify and work through their lessons as well. Enlightened leaders try to look for the silver lining within every cloud and see life's lessons as an opportunity for growth and self-expression for themselves and others.

You may find it helpful to remember that enlightened leaders

- Use their professional and personal experiences to grow as human beings
- Understand that our life experiences create the opportunity for our own spiritual growth
- See problems as opportunities in disguise
- Discover the silver linings in the clouds of life
- Strive to master life lessons in their easiest form
- Know that the weaknesses within our own strengths hold a key to understanding some of our life lessons
- Understand that each lesson mastered opens the gateway to the next lesson
- Understand that each ending creates the opportunity for a new beginning

KEY SIX: THE PRINCIPLE OF A HOLISTIC PERSPECTIVE

Perhaps you've heard the story about the three blind men who encountered an elephant. As the story goes, one reached out and caught the tail, one grabbed hold of a leg, and the third grasped the elephant's trunk. The first blind man thought he was touching a vine, the second a tree trunk, and the third a large snake. The problem, of course, was that each had a limited perspective, and none could see how the parts were related to the whole.

Leaders are inevitably dealing with people who perceive only one part of the elephant. Your job is not only to see the whole and how the parts contribute to it but also to help others see it. Think of this in terms of connections and context. Having the vantage point of a leader, you are in a position not only to see the connections but also to *create* them. Your job is to create the structures that bring people together for collaboration and to open the communication pathways in all directions. By bringing diverse elements of your organization together for dialogue and by setting a tone of mutual respect, you can help people gain a more holistic perspective on the issues that confront them. In your leadership role, you get to set the context or framework for whatever is unfolding. And you always want to do that from the highest perspective—a perspective that asks people to look at the whole, to look at the parts, and to look at the relationship of the parts to each other and to the whole.

As you know, people want to be meaningfully involved in decisions that affect their lives. You need to create processes that let the people who see the tail talk with both the people who see the trunk and the people who see the legs. When you also help them to ask questions from a holistic perspective regarding the way these elements affect each other and relate to the whole, staff members are more likely to realize they are working with an elephant. To put it another way, when people begin to see

We are complex beings composed of mind, body, and spirit. For our best selves to emerge, we must nurture and balance these three aspects.

holistically, they tend to be more understanding of diverse perspectives. In addition, when people are involved in meaningful ways in collaborative processes, this helps create positive, long-term institutional memory of both the process and the outcomes.

Leaders work with systems in which the components are connected and affect one another. People tend to see things from their own perspective. It's your job to help people see things from a larger, more holistic perspective.

The book *Appreciative Leaders* (edited by Marjorie Schiller, Deanna Riley, & Bea Mah Holland, 2001) has a subtitle: "In the Eye of the Beholder." We are convinced that many of the problems in education stem from the fact that some beholders have such a limited perspective. This is especially true with respect to the issue of governance, which from a holistic perspective affects everything else. As a leader, you must strive to help people see things from more than one perspective, which requires more openness and more collaboration. You might benefit from the wisdom expressed by Atticus Finch, played by Gregory Peck in the movie *To Kill a Mockingbird:* "You never really know a man until you stand in his shoes and walk around in them." Once you can see things as though you are standing in other people's shoes, you can help others do it, too.

Although putting yourself in the shoes of another may be useful, we have found that one of the best strategies is to ask people, "What does this look like through your eyes?" We are frequently surprised by what they say. When they tell us what it looks like through their eyes, we may not agree with their perspective, but it is one of the best ways we know for getting a true sense of other people's perspective. Understanding the other person's point of view may or may not help you to find common ground, but at the very least, communication will be enhanced, and the other person will have a sense that he or she has been heard.

A spiritual truth for people and organizations—indeed, for the Universe—is that the parts affect the whole and the whole affects the parts. Since we are part of the whole, it is in our own enlightened self-interest to devote our vision, energy, and gifts to shaping the world that is unfolding.

We are complex beings composed of mind, body, and spirit. For our best selves to emerge, we must nurture and balance these three aspects. Enlightened leaders nurture and balance these characteristics in themselves and in others. They see the mysterious interconnectedness of everything in the Universe and seek to understand how the parts of any system affect each other.

Enlightened leaders know that what we think, say, and do affects the Universe and what affects the Universe affects us. They know that for any system to operate effectively and efficiently, all of the parts must be able to work well individually and work well together.

Enlightened leaders help others recognize not only that they are part of something larger than themselves, but also that every part is vital and important to the success of the whole.

> You may find it helpful to remember that enlightened leaders
>
> - Strive to have a holistic perspective
> - Are aware that everything is connected
> - Understand that small changes can create large effects
> - Understand how the parts and the whole are related
> - Identify patterns so that others are able to see them
> - Model holistic thinking

KEY SEVEN: THE PRINCIPLE OF OPENNESS

Openness is a state of mind, an attitude toward people, ideas, and circumstances. It is the key to our growth as human beings. People are thought of as being generally open or closed, and so are organizations and societies. A person's degree of openness may fluctuate; you may be more open in some aspects of your life than in others, or more open at some times in your life than at others. It is not easy to be open because it makes you feel vulnerable and may, in fact, increase your vulnerability.

Openness is complex—openness to whom, openness to what, and under what circumstances? Openness involves letting things in, especially things you don't want to hear, and letting things out, as in openly speaking your truth, especially when it is not popular or good politics.

We subscribe to the notion that enlightened leaders strive to evolve in the direction of openness. Leaders should strive to open their minds to see as many possibilities as they can. They should strive to open their hearts to feel compassion, empathy,

When you model openness as a leader, you begin to influence your organization to develop a climate of openness. Creativity thrives in open climates—freedom thrives—and there is more joy and spontaneity.

and love. And they should strive to open their spirits to the full expression of who they really are. These are lofty goals, but openness happens bit by bit, moment by moment, choice by choice.

When you model openness as a leader, you begin to influence your organization to develop a climate of openness. People know whether they are in an open climate or a closed one. Creativity thrives in open climates—freedom thrives—and there is more joy and spontaneity. Open systems are organic; they grow and evolve. Closed systems are stifling; they stagnate and wither.

When you're not open in areas where you need to be more open, the world tends to let you know—there is a natural feedback system. Ironically, you can be open or closed to the feedback that is telling you to be more open, more flexible. You can always close the door to openness, but there is usually a price—your difficulties increase or your pain increases, and you may blame others or external events for this. It has been our experience that the last place most people look for the causes contributing to their difficulties is at themselves.

We often refer to the issue of openness because, in many ways, it is the prerequisite that allows the other spiritual principles of leadership to come forward. People are so different from each other in terms of where they fall on the continuum of openness. Where you fall on that continuum has a lot to do with the quality of your own life because, generally, you either don't let in much or you let in a great deal. By not allowing things in, you close yourself off from all sorts of potential connections and magic. On the other hand, if you are open, then synchronicity can happen, connections can be made, your connection to your higher self can happen—all those things can come about by being on the more open end of the continuum.

To us, openness is also a prerequisite for almost any kind of a fulfilled life. For leaders, it becomes even more critical; without openness, you are closing off your organization and the people you work with—not just yourself—and you are creating a dynamic that is extremely unhealthy. *Openness takes work.* As you nurture that in yourself as a leader, you open up your organization to greater possibilities.

Enlightened leaders appreciate openness in themselves and others. They try to be open to all aspects of themselves, to their environment, to the divine aspects of other people, and to the divine in themselves.

The Universe is pulsating with limitless information. It comes to us at conscious and unconscious levels, in direct and indirect ways. Information comes through our senses, through our dreams and intuition, through synchronicity, and through divine sources. Are we receptive to this information? Do we take advantage of it? We must struggle with forces such as fear, illness, and stress that push us to be closed rather than open.

Enlightened leaders work not only at hearing their own inner voice, but also at hearing the voices of others. Through wisdom, enlightened leaders learn to discern which voices and which information carry the highest truths and which carry lesser truths or untruths. It's not easy because sometimes the truth is unpleasant or painful or it means we have more work to do, but enlightened leaders continually work at being open to divine guidance to pursue the highest good.

You may find it helpful to remember that enlightened leaders

- See openness as a fundamental principle of leadership
- Foster openness in themselves and others
- Are open to seeing the divine qualities in themselves and others
- Seek to create and support open systems
- Are open to others
- Are open to life
- Are open to the spiritual dimension of life
- Strive to have an open heart
- Strive to have an open mind
- Help others to have open hearts and minds
- Use openness to foster their own growth and the growth of others
- Use openness to foster their own creativity and the creativity of others
- See openness as a key to creating infinite potentiality in themselves and others

---

KEY EIGHT: THE PRINCIPLE OF TRUST

With respect to the spiritual dimension of leadership, there may not be anything more important than being trusting. It is hard to be positive or to have reverence if you are not trusting. Paramount to everything else, trust implies a sense of openness, of possibility, of acceptance, of detachment The doorway of enlightened leadership opens through being trusting. Being trusting is the foundation of enlightened leadership, on which the other floors are built. If you can't trust, it becomes difficult to practice and express the other spiritual principles of leadership. We are struck by how little trust there is among the leaders we meet. We are always hearing talk about how they have to do various things because they really can't trust people. There seems to be a perception that you have to guard against other people, you have to protect yourself, and you have to create boundaries and walls because, without those, you can't function. But every wall you build is a wall against trust. Every door you close and lock is a door against trust. Nonetheless, trust is where you must start.

If you are among those who believe that everyone has a divine spark, then a place to start is to trust that it is there. Furthermore, embedded in that divine spark is an innate quality of goodness. You can trust that people are innately good and treat them accordingly; you can use trust to nurture the inherent goodness and divine spark in people. The very act of trusting people unleashes a powerful force that empowers them and brings out the best in them. Trust, then, is the recognition of the divine in someone else. Ultimately, that is what you are trusting: the higher self of those with whom you come in contact every day. You are not trusting their lower, ego-centered self because lower selves aren't very trustworthy—that's why they are lower.

When you interact with people, you choose what level you want to interact on, and they choose what level to respond on. The choice is simply to choose the higher self—which is divine, and therefore much easier to trust—or the lower self, which is more base and therefore much harder to trust. Everyone has both sides; metaphorically, everyone lives in a two-story house. Do you want to go to the top floor or the bottom floor? That is the choice. When you are interacting with another person, you choose on which floor to be. *Trust is about the choice you make, not about the other person.* It is more about you being trusting than about the other person being trustworthy. When you initiate trusting energy and trusting behavior, it tends to bring out the trustworthy parts in the other person. If the person wants to interact with you, and you are going to live on the second floor, he or she has got to join you there. Most people are capable of climbing the stairs. We know that there are exceptions; we've dealt with a few people over the years who were incapable of leaving the bottom floor. But if you choose to go up to that higher floor, most folks will join you there most of the time. Some people may not respond as you hope or they may stay on the bottom floor (responding to their lower self), but it is important not to generalize from that—not to say, "Well, that proves what happens when you trust someone."

We subscribe to the values expressed in the following quote, which has been attributed to Mother Teresa.

> People are often unreasonable, illogical, and self-centered; forgive them anyway. If you are kind, people may accuse you of selfish, ulterior motives; be kind anyway. If you are successful, you will win some false friends and some true enemies; succeed anyway. If you are honest and frank, people may cheat you; be honest and frank anyway. What you spend years building, someone may destroy overnight; build anyway. If you find serenity and happiness, they may be jealous; be happy anyway. The good you do today, people will often forget tomorrow; do good anyway. Give the world the best you have, and it may never be enough; give the world the best you've got anyway. You see, in the final analysis, it is all between you and God; it was never between you and them anyway.

The whole thrust of the quote is that you have a choice. Bad things may happen, but do the good thing anyway. People may disappoint you, but choose the higher road anyway. It is a powerful quote and exactly right because the choice is always yours. You have a choice to make about how you approach things. Do you choose to trust or not to trust? We have always tried to choose the trusting approach. What we have found is that 9 times out of 10, people will respond in a trustworthy manner. One time out of 10, they will not, and in those cases, you may be hurt or damaged. Give us odds of nine to one anytime, and we are going to take them. How about you?

We trust leaders who are authentic, leaders whose walk is aligned with their talk. We trust people who do what they say and say what they really do.

Trust is an essential principle for enlightened leaders—a principle that must begin within us. First, we must learn to trust ourselves and to be trustworthy. Then we have to learn to trust others and to give trust to others as a gift. Last, we must learn to trust the Universe, a higher spiritual power.

But trusting ourselves is not always easy. Trust must be tempered by wisdom to avoid trusting the wrong people or to protect against people betraying our trust. We trust leaders who are authentic, leaders whose walk is aligned with their talk. We trust people who do what they say and say what they really do.

Trust allows people to learn and grow although they may err along the way. Trust means living our integrity and respecting the integrity in others. Enlightened leaders tend to trust more so than not; when in doubt, they are more likely to choose to trust rather than choose not to trust.

You may find it helpful to remember that enlightened leaders

- Are trustworthy
- Trust themselves
- Are trusting
- Trust their higher self
- Trust the Universe
- Give trust as a gift

APPLYING THESE PRINCIPLES

Because the principles that we have tried to illuminate in this chapter are straightforward and easy to understand, it is easy to underestimate their importance, power, and depth. In the same way that things are easier said than done, these principles are easier read than done. These principles are like spiritual muscles; like our physical muscles, not only must they be used regularly, they also have to be exercised in order to strengthen them and increase their agility. The more you embrace these principles and practice them, the greater the payoff will be—not only for yourself and for those you lead, but ultimately for the entire world.

If you are committed to the principles associated with "The Spiritual Dimension of Leadership"—intention, attention, unique gifts and talents, gratitude, unique life lessons, a holistic perspective, openness, and trust—and you continually view these principles through the lens of spirituality, you will find that you are becoming a more enlightened leader—a leader who does the right things, in the right way, at the right time, all for the right reasons. Enlightened leadership is not an end in itself. It is a means—a means of bringing more wisdom to the world and of shaping a better future for our organizations and the children we serve.

Suggestions for Action

- Select one of the spiritual principles of leadership to personally embrace, express, and embody during an established time frame.
- Have each member of your leadership team select one of the spiritual principles of leadership to embrace, express, and embody during an established time frame.
- Have each school or department select one of the spiritual principles of leadership to embrace, express, and embody during a particular time frame.
- Have staff members generate and share stories that exemplify selected spiritual principles of leadership in practice.
- Create dialogue teams of three or more people who have selected the same spiritual principle of leadership to embrace, express, and embody during an established time frame.
- Have staff members work collaboratively to create action plans to implement one of the spiritual principles of leadership.
- Create teams of people who have selected the same spiritual principle of leadership to provide feedback and support to one another during the implementation process.
- Have staff members keep a reflective journal capturing their experience of embracing, expressing, and embodying one of the spiritual principles of leadership.
- Have staff members use their creativity to share the outcomes of embracing, expressing, and embodying one of the spiritual principles of leadership in their school or department.
- On a quarterly, semi-annual, or annual basis, select additional spiritual principles of leadership to embrace, express, and embody.

We have established a center that will serve as an information network, a support network, and a forum for collaboration and training, for everyone who is striving to become a more enlightened leader. If you are interested in learning more about the spiritual principles of leadership, you can contact us at the Center for Empowered Leadership (www.cfel.org).

May we enlighten our own and each other's paths.

REFERENCES

Myss, C. M. (2001). *Sacred contracts*. New York: Harmony Books.

Schiller, M., Riley, D., & Holland, B. M. (2001). *Appreciative leaders: In the eye of the beholder*. Chagrin Falls, OH: Taos Institute.

CHAPTER THREE

SPIRITUAL COURAGE

Leading From the Inside Out

DAWNA MARKOVA

We cultivate wisdom in our lives through widening our periphery and wondering our way through beautiful and dangerous questions. Wonder is not a disorder, deficit, or a waste of our time. It is one of our birthrights, one of our natural freedoms. It is how we can come to our senses in order to find and follow the meaning we want to make with the moments we have been given. It is the way we can think ourselves home. And home is the most natural place to risk reaching toward the world in a significant way.

—Dawna Markova

I was preparing to give a keynote speech to a large group of educational leaders. I asked Paul Houston to give me a sense of who would be in the room and what they most needed to hear from me. Without hesitation, he described the audience as a band of angels and saints who were struggling in turbulent and divisive times. He said they were being eaten alive by unions, school boards, parents, and politicians demanding accountability to standardized norms that left every child behind. Many were leaving the profession, bereft of their dreams, unsure of what would come next. He asked me to help them reclaim their dreams of a possible future and the courage to lead others from that dark place.

In my professional life, as an educator and thinking partner to organizational leaders, many initiatives, methodologies, and processes have come and gone. Everything works, and nothing works for very long. As a classroom teacher and learning specialist, I thought I was helping children at risk discover how they learn. As a clinical psychologist, I thought I was helping people who have been abused and have been challenged by disease and disruption liberate themselves from the limitations of their previous history. As an advisor to corporate executives, I thought I was helping organizations discover how to recognize and mobilize their intellectual capital. As a senior research affiliate, I thought I was exploring and teaching processes that expand the capacities we need to think really well together, to think through our right brains, our left brains, our hearts, minds, and bodies.

I have been doing all of these things—but underneath, I realize now, I was also learning to offer to others a simple and profound gift that author and "educator-at-large" Parker Palmer shared with me a decade ago: I was learning to listen people into speech, learning to help people turn inward in order to recognize and follow the narratives and questions that exist at the center of their lives.

The morning of that keynote address, I stood among the clumps of educational leaders having a continental breakfast outside the main hall. I walked around eavesdropping—listening not to specific conversations, but to the unspoken stories and questions that were right below the surface. Underneath the rush of words about curriculum and legislation, I heard a collective current of inquiry that sounded something like this:

We are doing more, and it is meaning less. How do we create coherence in this chaotic life? In this blur I can't see what matters. I can only see what is the matter—with the world, with myself, with my work. I can only see problems, what calls to be fixed, to be measured, to be solved. We are stuck in a corner between endless "eithers" and "ors." Ultimately, I am either frenzied or collapsed.

Thresholds of the Possible

This is an age of "narrative dysfunction." We have lost track of the story of ourselves, the stories that told us who we are supposed to be and how we are supposed to live.

—C. K. Williams

We are a fulcrum generation. We live, all of us, with one foot in the past and one in the future, in a house built over a fault line. The growing failure of our personal and cultural myths widens a crevice in each one of us. The support beams are giving way, because we have undermined the stories that brought them into proper alignment and bound them together. Those stories told us what it meant to be a woman, a man, a family; a member of a church, an organization, or a nation that would take care of you.

Every fairy tale used to begin with the words, "Once upon a time . . ." and end with "happily ever after." Before our generation, these stories, and indeed all the cultural myths we lived with, were never questioned. People weren't even aware there *were* stories. They lived in a world of givens and unquestioned

We live, all of us, with one foot in the past and one in the future, in a house built over a fault line. The growing failure of our personal and cultural myths widens a crevice in each one of us.

assumptions that directed them. Everyone played the game more or less by the same rules—work hard enough and you would progress—and expected the same prize: security. The world was easily divided into Good and Bad, Black Hats and White Hats, Us and Them. We were expected to live in one place, be married to one person, have one job, one parent of each gender, one common destination, and one God. The certainty of misery was definitely preferred to the misery of uncertainty.

These stories we shared were guiding images that required a culture high in continuity and control. In this time of immense flux and chaos, however, people on a large scale are refusing to give their power away to an abstract—be it company or nation or government—that in the end is only made of human beings. We are coming to accept that no Big Daddy is going to make everything all right, and thus are refusing relationships that involve domination. We are insisting on adult-to-adult interactions. All false boundaries are coming down. We are beginning to recognize that we cannot sustain life if we continue to think in a way that pits ideas against action, actions against feelings, feelings against thinking, and the past against the future.

Those of us who consider ourselves educational leaders have been part of the unraveling of the dominator mythology of power, of command and control, of walls that separate and ladders that you climb to places you never wanted to go in the first place. We are disenchanted as we begin this millennium, and have tried to hold on by putting new people in the old roles. However, disenchantment has decayed into cynicism and finally crumbled into disillusionment— letting go of the old stories altogether, and our passion and inspiration along with them. Disillusionment, however, need not be a bad thing, for imagination begins where the old stories hit a wall.

Disillusionment can feel like dying. What *was* is falling apart in some deep way, as if a shedding were taking place, but what *will be* has not yet emerged. I've been told that as it is about to shed its skin, the eyes of a snake turn milky white, leaving it temporarily blind. The creature then withdraws into the familiar darkness of its burrow, waiting for its new skin to grow. If we are to make it through this time of shedding, we need to be guided by the wisdom of all natural creatures. We need to reclaim our comfort with the unknown. We need to move beyond the fear of our own imagination.

As educational leaders, we need our imagination to create new stories that will unify us. No longer are we inspired by a warrior stepping out to do battle with a sword. Instead we must learn, somehow, to step out *without* armor, to participate in transformation through relationship and inquiry. We must find transnational ways to define who we are. Our old stories are not big enough for what we must do now. Like so many of the characters in the fairy tales, we are lost in a dark wood with only the small flame of our spirit to light the way.

Being lost can bring you fully alive, though, alert to every intersection that might hold a clue to tell you where you are. It is a time to come to your senses, to notice where you are in acute detail. It is a time to sort out whether the sound you hear is actually a bear or merely your own stomach growling. Being lost can help you become aware of the stories you tell yourself that determine who you think you are, how you connect or don't to the world as a whole, and whether or not you think the universe is a friendly place.

What has never been understood so fully before is that we coauthor our future. Life doesn't just happen *to* us; we inhabit a participatory universe, influencing and being influenced on a cellular level by everything around us. We know now that we are not simply parts of a machine, and that the greatest gift we can offer is the use of our consciousness to transform our experience. However, we cannot have conversations about cocreating a possible future for the world if we don't each have courageous conversations with our own spirit about how we can recreate our personal destiny.

THE CRUCIBLE OF THE UNKNOWN

> *You must have a place in your heart, your mind, your house, your day, where you can go and where you do not know what you owe anyone or what anyone owes you.*

> —Joseph Campbell

The most abused and underused resource we have available to us at this time is human imagination. It is as if we are all born with two arms—our capacity to think in the rational domain and our capacity to imagine and think relationally. In our linear culture, however, living with one arm tied behind our backs is considered normal. Most of us have even forgotten that we have thus handicapped ourselves. In order to create a future that we would want to live in, we need to reclaim our imagination as a strategic force so that we no longer narcotize ourselves into believing that lives that diminish and fragment us are the way things must be.

I once visited an 8-year-old girl in her second-grade classroom. The teacher had told me she had attention deficit disorder. When I knelt down beside her desk as she was staring out the window during a creative writing period, she whispered, "It's just that my imagination keeps getting in the way."

We live in a time when most of

In order to be comfortable in the enormous change and unknown future that presents itself at every corner of the outer world, we must relearn to become comfortable with the inner aspect of ourselves that feels lost.

us are used to having our imagining done *for* us. Members of a leadership team in an educational system for which I was consulting complained that they were having difficulty creating a shared vision. When I asked how I could help, they explained that I should come up with the vision for them, and then they could react to it. They did not realize that they could not hope to capture the imagination of their community without recapturing their own. Current research on learning indicates that we have the capacity to think in many ways, using so many modes: rational and relational, factual and mythological, analysis and synthesis. The human mind that has created so much suffering in the last century is also the mind that is capable of healing it.

In order to be comfortable in the enormous change and unknown future that presents itself at every corner of the outer world, we must relearn to become comfortable with the inner aspect of ourselves that feels lost. If we are bereft of our relationship with the unknown, we cannot be aware of what stories are trying to be born in us at any given moment. We live on the surface of our lives, losing connection with our miraculous capacity to regenerate ourselves through our imagination.

THE TYRANNY AND GLORY OF THE IMAGINATION

Stories are our nearest and dearest way of understanding our lives and finding our way onward.

—Ursula K. LeGuin

Stories are much more than entertainment. They gather our experience into shapes, in much the same way that a fish tank gives form to the watery reality of a goldfish. Researchers place them at the foundation of memory and learning. Stories provide the meaning that structures our lives; they take individual moments and place them in a cohesive movement. Whether we tell them publicly to others or murmur them secretly to ourselves, stories fuel the engine of our desire and generate our actions.

And most of us, like the fish in the water, are not even aware of them. Several years ago I was working with a renowned professor of psychology. Within minutes of entering my office, he lit a carved pipe and began to tell me stories. The conversation went something like this: "Dr. Markova, you must understand that I am not a very creative person. I'm extraordinarily analytic, left-brained, actually. . . . You, on the other hand, are very imaginative, which I am definitely not. If we are to work on this project together, you're going to have to validate your reasoning in an appropriate manner. . . ."

The facts of this experience were as follows: He entered the room, shook my hand, sat down, lit his pipe, looked at me, and tightened his jaw. I asked him how he knew I was very imaginative. He shrugged, puffed on his pipe, and said he could just tell. After much inquiry, his final response was, "You are of Russian ancestry, as was my mother. *She* was very creative, so I imagine you are too." When examined from outside the tank, the facts were that his mother and I had a similar genetic background. Everything else was story. And all of this from a "not very creative" person! Once the professor became aware of the stories he told himself much of the time, he began to realize that he was the author of his own existence.

I'd like to invite you to pause for a few moments and discover some of your own personal mythology: For a moment or two, scribble down the facts of your current reality. For example, you might say, "I'm sitting in a green chair, my legs crossed, reading page 43 of this book." Observe the landscape of your thinking as you write, as if a part of you were a witness sitting on your shoulder. You'll soon notice the terrain starts to take on a specific shape. For instance, you might notice yourself saying, "I'm sitting in this green chair, reading, and noticing that it's getting late and I'd better make dinner." Imagine an invisible witness asking you, "What story are you telling yourself about that?" Your response, when you pause to notice, might be something like, "I glanced at the clock and told myself that I was lazy sitting here reading for so long, while there was important work to do." This brief but potent story reinforces a belief about yourself (lazy if not coerced into action), your purpose (to provide), and your relationship to the world (as long as you're taking care of the work, you belong).

These internal, constantly playing, invisible narratives form the strategy of our imagination. They are essential tools of personal identity and community building since they tell us, individually and collectively, who we are; what our purpose is; and how we connect, or don't, to the whole. As soon as we join the human community, people start shoving stories into us as if they were software disks: "Oh, isn't he a cute baby? He's colicky, isn't he? Probably he has a delicate constitution just like his Uncle Bob." Or we hear stories like, "Everyone knows that the human race is basically hostile and aggressive." Like the DNA in our cells, these myths teach us how to be human by shaping and passing on our best and worst qualities.

NOT ALL STORIES ARE CREATED EQUAL

When people come to see me, their problem is that they experience life as the same damn thing over and over. If we've been successful, when we're finished with our work together, they perceive it as one damn thing after another.

—Carl Whittaker, MD

As with any great force of nature, there is both danger and glory in the stories we tell ourselves and each other. Some of these myths rally against understanding; others promote it. Some are toxic and keep our problems festering; others are tonic, bringing us into healing. Some have the potential to expand possibilities, and some to limit them. To be in a life of our own definition, we must be able to discover which scenarios we are following and whether they help us grow the forms that offer us the most interesting possibilities.

To do this, we need to differentiate between what I call *rut stories*—the inferences, beliefs, assessments, and assumptions we hold that tranquilize us into passivity—and *river stories*—those that energize us into exploring the current of our lives through all its tributaries.

Rut stories tell you. You tell river stories.

There are four basic categories of rut stories: impossibility ("You can't fight city hall"), invalidation ("I'm just not a sensitive kind of person."), blame ("My family life is shot because the company expects me to work 80-hour weeks."), and nonaccountability ("I'm in Accounting—let HR deal with personnel problems."). Since everything in nature has its balancing counterpart, there are also four categories of river stories: possibility ("I wonder what I could do differently to make this happen."), validation ("I certainly have learned how to organize my life; I am curious to discover how I could become more aware of people's feelings."), choice ("Even though everyone else works too much, I'm just not going to do it—my family is too important to me."), and accountability ("Even though it's not my job, I know a lot of people in HR—I'll see to it that someone takes care of this problem.").

Rut stories tell you. You tell river stories. The easiest way to discern them is to choose a moment or two on a regular basis to step outside your habits of thought and ask an open question such as

"Whom or what am I serving now?" or "What am I dedicating these moments to now?" Then notice the stories you are telling yourself. Do they leave you feeling numb, zoned out, energized?

Several years ago, I was diagnosed with cancer. I discovered that the rut stories I heard about the illness were as much an assault from the outside "expertocracy" as the cancer cells were from the inside: "This is your diagnosis. The form of cancer you have is incurable. It will kill you. There's nothing anyone can do." Or, "You are responsible for creating your own reality." Each time I sat down to imagine my system healing, those rut stories reinforced the ones I had carried for most of my life: "Who am I to think I could heal from this? No one ever has. I've never been very physical anyway. I'm constitutionally inadequate. If I had expressed my anger, this never would have happened."

Be it ever so toxic, there's no place like a rut story. I had been putting myself to bed with them, waking up to them, and playing them as the top-10 tunes on my mental radio for most of my life. They were the hand-me-downs and heirlooms of some of my kith and kin. They were killing me. But without them, all I had was my human helplessness and congenital fear of the unknown.

Then I read a book that changed everything: *Man's Search for Meaning,* by psychologist Victor Frankl, written about his experiences in a concentration camp. In those pages, I learned that no one could take away my personal freedom—the meaning I ascribed to any event that happened to me. If I could learn to be comfortable in the unknown, I could choose which stories I told myself about cancer, what I was and was not capable of doing, and what I was and was not responsible for.

If you are willing to engage in this same process with courageous curiosity, you will have taken a significant step in freeing yourself from harmful family and cultural patterns that have limited your growth and giving. You will also have added to the mercy in the world. The more we all move from limiting diagnoses and narratives to liberating ones, the freer and more energized our collective imagination will become to create a possible future.

FROM THE RUT TO THE RIVER

I don't know Who—or What—put the question, I don't know when it was put. I don't even remember answering. But at

*some moment I did answer Yes to Someone—or Something—
and from that hour I was certain that existence is meaningful and that, therefore, my life, in self-surrender, had a goal.*

—Dag Hammarskjöld

What if you thought of yourself like the moon, and had the same
degree of faith in what was ready to fade away and what was invisible as you did in what was shining? What if you let go of the known
and comfortably habitual ways of thinking about yourself and the
world and engaged with what is dormant within you? What if, instead
of assuming you were depressed or falling apart, you gave yourself
3 days a month or 3 hours a day to allow everything you know about
yourself to disappear? Giving yourself this opportunity to engage in
innocent inquiry with who you are and what you are becoming creates a rich and dark soil for regeneration.

The capacity we have that supports this transformation is called
awareness or mindfulness. In effect, it is a process of widening one's
periphery. Scientists know that when we go into a fight-or-flight
response, we narrow ourselves into "tunnel vision." This affects
much more than our vision, however. All of our senses become nar-
rowed. We can only perceive how we are stuck. Think of a day
recently when you were "in crisis." How much of the world around
you did you actually notice?

In order to liberate yourself, it is necessary to reverse the process.
Ask yourself some evocative questions that have no one right
answer, such as, "I recognize my work is too small for me. I wonder
what I could do that would bring me alive" Or, "I'm just going
through the motions with my kids. I wonder what I need to be doing
so that I'm actually enjoying them again."

Then do nothing except get curious and widen your periphery.
When we notice what is—without *trying* to change it, fix it, or judge
it—we establish a feedback loop with our own experience that
enables us to choose the most natural direction in which to change.
This is how we learn naturally. It is how a baby learns to walk.

DEEPER MOMENTS, WIDER HORIZONS

*Let yourself be silently drawn by the stronger pull of what
you really love.*

—Rumi

Just as geese have an internal capacity to follow coastlines and the magnetic resonance of the Earth to tell them where to go, just as bats can echo-locate to find their direction, so you can begin to trust your own inner resources to guide you through the tributaries of your own river stories.

You don't have to become an optimist or recite programmed affirmations to find a river story. Become a *possibilist.* Imagine that which you seek is floating somewhere around you. Every river begins and ends in the ocean. All of your life has been moving toward it. All of evolutionary intelligence is supporting its emergence, because you are unique. Your gift lies in what you love, and the whole human community needs you to bring that gift to it.

Your gift lies in what you love, and the whole human community needs you to bring that gift to it.

Your job is to be quiet and alone from time to time, asking the open questions that have no answers and letting them drift in the winds of your mind like a kite. Often this means reestablishing a relationship with your own silence so that you will be patient enough with yourself to allow the most interesting possibilities of your spirit to emerge.

Analytic modes of thinking will often lead you to your deficits—the mistakes and missteps you have taken in your past while trying to follow the rules. But the wider, systemic way of reflecting that I'm suggesting searches for exceptions to the rules. Since you are holding the string of the kite, you can direct it back to your assets, to other moments in your life when you have been successful and felt fulfilled meeting challenges or trusted your own wisdom. You might recall a time when you found the way to express what had heart and meaning for you. What did you look like at that moment? How did you sound? How were you moving? What were the sensations in your body?

There is also an inner resource I call "following in their footsteps." If you cannot access a time when you expressed your authentic truth in a similar situation to the one you are facing, you can imagine how one of the great souls of your life would do it. You might call on the vivid memory or image of a mentor you respect deeply and notice in great detail how he or she would look, sound, move, and feel in your circumstance. Similarly, you can also invoke an older, wiser, more authentic and practiced "you" of 5 years in the future who has made it. You can then follow, step by step, the path they mark.

Each of Us Creates for All of Us

Our lives begin to end the day we become silent about the things that really matter.

—Dr. Martin Luther King, Jr.

All of us have experienced fragmentation that has limited our past and threatens our future. There are many forces that are trying to convince us more of our separation than of our connection. The journey from rut to river increases the porosity of the membranes that divide us from our own spirit and from each other.

As we wonder ourselves forward, we can choose to engage in the kind of inquiry, individually and collectively, that encourages "leaky margins": Who is there that I will not allow myself to learn with? What do I love so much that in the doing of it I find a kind of grace in the world? What are the ways of working and relating that bring me alive? How can I move the pivot of my existence so that I am serving a finer purpose? What is it that if I don't say it, I die a little each day? Who are the people and what are the conditions that bring out the best in me? How do I risk becoming more real and more alive? What will liberate my heart?

Questions such as these have no one right answer. They become companions that draw you forward, connecting you to your heart. They are allies in the unknown, thresholds to the possible.

We may or may not be able to change the world, but it is within the sphere of influence of every person reading these words to choose to create a new personal mythology of active engagement with our present and future. Being between stories, we are leaving behind patterns of thinking that have limited human possibility for generations. We are also at a wonderful beginning—a second innocence, perhaps—where we can use our consciousness to realize the dreams of all those who have nourished, protected, and passed on their life to us.

We are supported, perhaps guided, by an evolutionary intelligence that has carried us from the age of handcrafting through the age of the machine and now—where? The information age? The age of mindcrafting? If we slip free of the too-small circles we have drawn around ourselves, if we allow ourselves permeable boundaries, moving from rut to river, we may discover that we are not as alone as we think. We may find that we are held and guided by hidden hands.

CHAPTER FOUR

APPRECIATIVE INQUIRY

A Strategy for Reshaping Education That Builds on Strengths and Hopes

BEA MAH HOLLAND

The future belongs to methods that affirm, compel, and accelerate anticipatory learning involving larger and larger levels of collectivity. . . . Instead of negativism, criticism, and spiraling diagnosis, there will be discovery, dream, and design.

—David Cooperrider, founder of Appreciative Inquiry
(as quoted in Whitney, 1996)

WHY USE APPRECIATIVE INQUIRY?

Imagine an approach to strengthening your workplace that is based on solutions that have worked, that is collaborative, and that harnesses the collective wisdom of *everyone*—not just those in traditional leadership roles, but representatives of every constituency with a stake in the outcome. Instead of repeating deeply ingrained patterns of "doing things the same old way and expecting different results," Appreciative Inquiry (AI) is a powerful opportunity to work in radically different ways—and to produce radically different results. While deceptively simple in its practice, AI has brought about noteworthy outcomes around the world in virtually every sector: business, health care, education, and both not-for-profit and government agencies. AI has been used in working with educational systems of every size: individuals in one-on-one coaching situations, groups of students, work teams, school districts, and entire communities that have committed themselves to educational transformation.

Appreciative Inquiry is a powerful opportunity to work in radically different ways—and to produce radically different results.

This chapter summarizes the origin, philosophy, and methodology of Appreciative Inquiry, then presents case examples of AI applications in educational settings. These include the coaching of a recently fired public school superintendent; a high school leadership development program for girls; work team interventions; and macro-level programs, including Maine's *Celebrate School People* and the University of Memphis College of Education's annual endeavor of bringing together 240 representatives of relevant constituencies to ensure that the institution fulfills its aspiration to stay "leading, relevant, and engaged."

In the early 1980s, David Cooperrider, then a PhD student at Case Western Reserve University, began researching how people in organizations could be most effective. At his research site at the Cleveland Clinic, he noticed that when he inquired about people's successes, strengths, values, and hopes, they experienced a palpable surge of power. Repeatedly observing this phenomenon, Cooperrider hypothesized,

> The most important thing we do as consultants is inquiry. . . . The key point is that *the way we know* is fateful. The questions we ask, the things that we choose to focus on, the topics that we choose determine what we find. What we find becomes the data and the story out of which we dialogue about and envision the future. And so the seeds of change are implicit in the very first

questions we ask. [Italics added] (Cooperrider, Stavros, & Whitney, 2003, p. 85)

Cooperrider's theory was reinforced by the positive psychology movement spearheaded by Martin Seligman, president of the American Psychological Association in the 1990s. Positive psychology is now widely accepted as a field of legitimate research, and the aligned findings have furthered the interest in and credibility accorded to Appreciative Inquiry as an approach to individual and organizational development. In 1997, the American Society for Training and Development (ASTD) recognized Appreciative Inquiry as the best organizational change program in the United States; in 2004, ASTD awarded Cooperrider the prestigious Distinguished Contribution to the Field of Workplace Learning and Performance Award.

PHILOSOPHY AND METHODOLOGY

Appreciative Inquiry is both a philosophy and a methodology. AI is based on the assumption that individuals, teams, organizations, and communities are replete with solutions—that all living systems have an untapped trove of successful experiences. Appreciative Inquiry encourages the explicit acknowledgment of the strengths, positive experiences, values, and aspirations of each individual, and then enables organizations to gather these assets and capitalize on this storehouse of collected and collective wealth. The attention to first clearly hearing individual strengths and yearnings makes organizational alignment more likely and serves as the springboard for the group's aspirations to emerge from the potent core of each individual.

The Appreciative Inquiry philosophy assumes an innate higher consciousness that can express itself in a safe, nurturing environment. Since individuals know that who they are and what they want have been given voice and incorporated into the collective thinking of those present, the sense of a "we" that strives for the accomplishment of the greater good can be embraced by all participants. People find meaning in serving something larger than themselves, and ego-driven needs for accolades and control lessen.

Appreciative Inquiry is based in spirit because it taps into the inner aspect of a person's highest consciousness. As noted by

St. Irenaeus, a theologian of the second century, "Man [and woman] fully alive is the Glory of God"—and people become reality as they become engaged mentally, physically, emotionally, and socially. Qualities such as enthusiasm, creativity, playfulness, connection, delight, and generosity are readily apparent when people participate in the cocreation of their common destiny. Anchored in the recognition and articulation of the unique assets that reside in each person, AI allows multiplication rather than addition to become the norm. "I–Thou" rather than "I–it" relationships are forged through the somewhat rare but invaluable appreciative process of focused, one-on-one inquiry and deep, attentive listening.

> *AI is based on the assumption that individuals, teams, organizations, and communities are replete with solutions—that all living systems have an untapped trove of successful experiences.*

This asset-based approach is grounded in several principles, including the following:

- Change begins the moment that inquiry begins.
- Our words create our worlds, so our way of thinking is directly related to what we do.
- We have a choice as to whether to explore problems or possibilities.
- Unconditionally positive questions lead to constructive change.

While perhaps more a philosophy than a methodology, an Appreciative Inquiry 4-D Cycle can serve as a framework for action (see Figure 4.1). The cycle—Discovery, Dream, Design, and Destiny—describes the process for moving forward, whether for an individual, a group of students, a work team, a community, a state, or a movement.

Discovery. In this beginning phase, people decide about the focus of the inquiry. What do they want to learn about? What would they like to know about the positive capacity of the individuals involved in the process? People, usually in pairs, interview one another to learn about high-point experiences, strengths, assets, and aspirations they hold for the future. In contrast to more typical strategies that analyze deficits, AI seeks the root causes of success through carefully worded questions. The focus is on "What's going right, and how do we get more of it?"

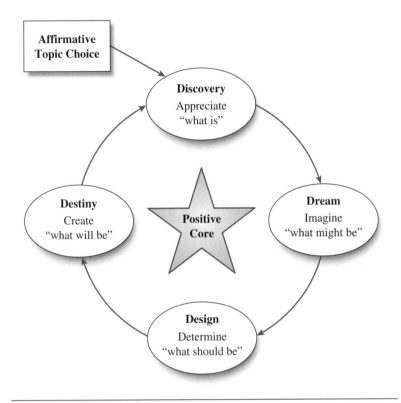

Figure 4.1   Appreciative Inquiry (AI) 4-D Cycle

Adapted from Cooperrider et al. (2003). *Appreciative Inquiry Handbook: The First in a Series of AI Workbooks for Leaders of Change*, p. 83. San Francisco: Berrett-Koehler.

Dream. The reflective Discovery conversations about one's unique experiences, gifts, and hopes lead to a collective image of an ideal future. Building on realized success stories that are grounded in people's positive histories, people come to see that best practices can be the norm, as they articulate their future dream-come-true workplace.

Design. This third phase of the 4-D cycle brings people together to design the system's structures and policies that will enable the manifestation of the collective dream. Together, people rigorously identify changes that they would like to make in their social architecture in order to move toward their collective ideal—modifications in their processes, roles, metrics, and systems.

Destiny. As people are pulled toward their future conception, they experiment. The individual and collective momentum affects the organization as people use their creativity, continuously inquiring as to what is working, what can be expanded, and what can be let go. An ongoing recursive process, the energy is focused on shared outcomes as people continue to discover, dream, and design.

The following education cases are all grounded in asset-based inquiries in which I have participated, most frequently as a facilitator-consultant. I served as one of the Appreciative Inquiry collaborators in the Waltham High School Girls Leadership Program and as a coconvener and coconsultant with the KnowledgeWorks Foundation in their dialogues about the purpose of education. In 2002, I was invited to train an open-enrollment AI program in Memphis; based on that work, I have cofacilitated the University of Memphis College of Education Summit annually since 2005. I was the keynote speaker in the Maine statewide program *Celebrating School People.* At Wheaton College in Norton, Massachusetts, I have been working as a sole consultant, and I served as the coach of the fired public school superintendent.

AI Interventions Contributing to Educational Transformation

1. Waltham High School Girls Leadership Program

What happens when we provide adolescents with opportunities to meet grown-ups who are actually living the adolescents' unrealized dreams? Such pursuits might seem far-fetched, given today's omnipresent emphasis on testing to meet Adequate Yearly Progress goals. Yet when Rosemary Neville, a housemaster of Waltham High School in Greater Boston, told me and fellow AI collaborators Muriel Finegold, Gabriela Canepa, and Lani Peterson her deep concerns about the underachievement, questionable life decisions, and school dropout rates of many of her young female students, we saw these conditions as prime territory for the implementation of an AI model program we called *Three Saturdays and a Wow!* The essence behind *Wow* was to provide a program that would meet the needs of high school girls at the margins. Our aims were to identify common ground, to empower and foster the girls' leadership, and to provide them with opportunities to interact with people who were living the embodiment of their dreams.

In the ensuing planning meetings, the AI collaborators realized that the invitation to these girls to voluntarily participate in *any* program would need to be unusually compelling. After reflecting on what might best match the goals of the program with the hearts of the potential attendees, housemaster Neville and the organizers decided to publicize the program for those girls who had a "spark of leadership."

Our aims were to identify common ground, to empower and foster the girls' leadership, and to provide them with opportunities to interact with people who were living the embodiment of their dreams.

Because the school year was already more than half over, the program was offered for 26 hours over three consecutive Saturdays, to be followed by a celebratory event. Through well-tuned orchestration among the headmaster, faculty, and organizers, 15 freshman girls—about half of them Latino and the rest a mix of white, African American, and Asian—showed up for the first meeting of *Three Saturdays and a Wow!*

Wow's first scheduled Saturday was greeted by the girls with noticeable skepticism. For some it may have been a rarity that someone had seen something positive in them—a "spark of leadership." In addition, their sometimes complex lives—both past and current— had left them with limited trust as well as withdrawn or acting-out behaviors. The program began gently, as the girls noticed sayings by Eleanor Roosevelt and Margaret Mead, among others, that were posted on the walls—quotations that had resonated with other adolescents. The girls were invited to stand by the poster that they felt any connection to and to discuss why they were drawn to that particular one. This provided an opportunity for each person to speak to the 14 other young women, whether in just two or three words or a few paragraphs. Each voice had now been heard.

After this icebreaker, the facilitators asked the girls to identify their hopes and fears by anonymously writing each of them on sticky notes, then posting their fears on one chart and their hopes on another. Volunteers read the two charts aloud. After seeing the range of hopes and fears that had been articulated, the girls realized that they had an enormous number of feelings of both fear and possibilities in common with each other.

The prototype AI methodology began with the Discovery phase, in which paired interviews and the invitation to tell stories immediately gave the girls self-understanding as to why others saw a spark of leadership in them. Every girl responded to questions in 15 minutes of structured paired interviewing. Each participant told her partner about how she had overcome obstacles and (with a nudge to speak about her strengths) articulated the particular skills, knowledge, and gifts that were part of her makeup.

In the subsequent debriefing, each girl introduced her partner to four girls, and then to the entire group. The young women again recognized commonalities they shared, including powerful feelings of being different, being shy, not fitting in, or feeling not smart enough. In the next breath, however, they spoke about their hopes and career aspirations, their courage, and their wit and strengths in overcoming major obstacles that included language, poverty, and complex family structures—sometimes with single parents, or no parents at all. Building on this successful experience of interviewing and having been interviewed, the facilitators asked each girl, during the coming week, to interview at least one or two female adults. The girls were asked to report the responses to specific interview questions at the next session.

Wow's second scheduled Saturday clearly had a different tenor from the previous meeting. The girls were upbeat and enthusiastic about sharing the information they had gathered during their interviews of relatives and close family friends. They told stories ranging from what it was like for a family to immigrate to America to how people they knew overcame obstacles to living success stories that involved realizing one's dreams.

Again, the revelation was realizing that most of their interviewees shared similar feelings of isolation and fear just as the girls themselves did but that, with continued perseverance, they were able to achieve remarkable success. The girls acknowledged new feelings of hope and confidence through learning what others had been through and how their ways of coping had paid off. Lani Peterson, a gifted storyteller who was one of the AI collaborators, coached the girls in telling their own unique stories.

This experience of interviewing people whom they knew served as a training ground for the final round of interviewing—this time involving professionals we had recruited from fields in which the girls were interested. The 15 girls eagerly collaborated on interview questions, and the agenda became set for *Wow*'s third scheduled Saturday.

This final session had an electric feeling—a feeling that had often eluded these girls in the past. Eleven amazing professional women agreed to share not only their Saturday, but also their stories of fear, marginality, shaken confidence, challenges, and, ultimately, success. The time flew by so quickly that not even lunch could interrupt the conversations in which the women and the girls were deeply immersed. The conversations were

The final session had an electric feeling—a feeling that had often eluded these girls in the past.

lively and, even more important, emphasized commonalties that these girls would previously not have believed were possible.

The city's mayor, for example, spoke about growing up in a housing project. A very confident African American attorney spoke about her problems in school and about being different. One of the 15 girls found inspiration through meeting two women who have used their artistic talents as a graphic facilitator and as a landscape architect. An aspiring teacher met with a former teacher and university professor who came in full Harvard regalia on her way to commencement exercises. Several of the women offered to advocate for and stay in touch with the girls. Afterward, the girls took exceptional care in thanking their interviewees with beautifully crafted handwritten notes.

The participants came together at a final *Wow* celebration, where they presented a summary of the Girls Leadership Program to their parents, siblings, and friends. Many of the girls have continued in their growth toward becoming healthy, independent, confident young women. This program has since been replicated with other high school students as well as with middle school students. The power of the Girls Leadership Program lies in guiding young women to experience that they are worthwhile persons who already have a spark of leadership and the capacity to become fully alive, powerful leaders— not "at-risk" individuals who need to be "fixed" by others. Through this program, each young woman gained an understanding of leadership as a process in which she leads *herself* through day-to-day challenges and continues in her appreciation of herself as a worthy person who has the capability to grow into a better version of herself.

How might you imagine incorporating programs of this nature in your school, your community, your city, your state, your country, and your world?

2. Maine's "Celebrate School People Day"

Imagine a 2,300-person event that celebrates all the people who work with schoolchildren—their bus drivers, crossing guards, teachers, cafeteria workers, principals, superintendents, custodians, social workers, coaches, education technicians, librarians, nurses, substitutes, administrative assistants, and all administrators. Picture a gathering where Los Angeles actor Mark Ruffalo—the star of *Rumor Has It, All the King's Men, Just Like Heaven,* and *Zodiac*—tearfully reunites with his life-changing high school English teacher, Lenora Antley from Virginia.

Visualize Noel Paul Stookey (of Peter, Paul, and Mary fame) conducting groups of school choruses singing "I'm on Air"—a song whose words he wrote specifically for this event, with music by Paul Sullivan, a Grammy Award–winning pianist and composer. Imagine the music as Noel and Paul conduct instrumentalists and singers as diverse as Pieces of String from Eastport and the Pihcintu Singers, a Maine choir of multicultural singers from 10 different countries. Witness Miss Maureen Corr, now 80-plus years old and formerly Eleanor Roosevelt's personal secretary, as she shares stories about the First Lady's commitment to education and her role in spearheading legislation for an "earlier" Celebrate School People event known as Teacher Appreciation Day.

The Augusta Civic Center in Maine was the place to be on October 18, 2006, with Maine's First Lady Karen Baldacci, Maine Commissioner of Education Susan Gendron, state representatives, educational leaders, and school people of all kinds gathering to recognize the work of a community of people who too often are taken for granted: workers in early childhood education, K–12 public and private schools, home schools, and institutions of higher education. Some 2,300 "school people" laughed, smiled, cried, and whispered to each other at this celebration that, for some, was the first time that they truly felt recognized for their loyal service to young people.

Several kickoff events in the spring of 2006 heralded the culminating fall gathering, including a press conference at the Statehouse Hall of Flags and a reception at the governor's Blaine House residence that was attended by representatives from Maine's congressional delegation. An official proclamation issued by Governor Baldacci was read, announcing October 18, 2006, as "Celebrate School People Day" in Maine. This same gathering featured the unveiling of a painting by artist Mary Byrom—a painting that captured the diversity of educational service providers ranging from cafeteria workers to the bus driver at North Berwick Elementary School. In preparation for the October 18 event, every school district in Maine held lotteries to determine four representatives to attend the gala, thus insuring statewide participation.

With 25 years of experience working in public schools, lead organizer Kathleen Alfiero and her collaborator, Patsy Wiggins, dreamed of an event that would acknowledge and celebrate the seemingly infinite dedication of "school people." Feeling the need to support and recognize all school service providers within the entire system— both the prominent as well as the virtually invisible—and trained in Appreciative Inquiry by David Cooperrider, Kathleen centered the celebration on stories told about school people's generosity of spirit with a simple appreciative inquiry: "Do you remember school people who believed in you and inspired you to be the best you can be?"

Kathleen's questions were posed in places as diverse as the Maine Mall, Bangor Mall, and Presque Isle Mall, the tiny island school of Matinicus Island, and communities throughout the state. The instigators videotaped stories from the perspective of students and former students, and from school people who, through fate and circumstance, were called to do extraordinary things with children.

At the Celebrate School People event, poet Kellie Wardman read her tribute titled "To Miss Welch, Grade 5," and Donna, an elementary principal, shared a letter of thanks to Mrs. Finks for saying to her many years ago, "You can be anything you want to be, Donna."

"SOMEBODY outside the profession saw that I and my colleagues had worth! . . . The day was my Heisman Trophy, my standing ovation."

Videotaped interviews—in conjunction with live interviews, reunions on stage, music, and other presentations—bombarded attendees at the celebration with the reminder of their extraordinary capacity to change lives. It was my privilege as a keynote speaker to remind school people, "In the whole world you may be only one person, but to one person you may be the whole world." Statewide and local television coverage as well as prolific newspaper coverage disseminated stories about school people and their impact.

What was the impact of this one afternoon program? Plenty! One male teacher said, "It was validating that SOMEBODY outside the profession saw that I and my colleagues had worth. An actor gets applause, an athlete gets trophies, but teachers get complaints, constraints, budget deficits, more and more students and more and more work. The day was my Heisman Trophy, my standing ovation."

Enga Stewart, the principal of Lincoln School, instituted an Adopt-a-Child Program as a result of attending the Celebrate School People event and reported,

> It was wonderful to be honored for our work in schools. My staff and I who attended enjoyed every minute of this professional production. On October 25, I challenged each of my staff to adopt a child not in their classroom, and to be sure to reach out and speak to that child at least every week. The staff meeting followed the Celebrate School People theme, "You may be only one person in the world, but you can be the world to one person." The staff was asked to (1) adopt a child, and (2) everyone greet the children, "Good morning! Welcome to school." Call the children by name. At our January 2, 2007, staff meeting I am asking staff to report out on their adopted student. . . . It was a wonderful experience and it does not end in attending the event. Our children are our future, and we need to continue to foster caring, kindness, respect. We, the adults in schools, are the role models for so many children. [The event] was superb and awe-inspiring as produced!

Recognizing that "In the whole world, you may be just one person, but to one person you may be the whole world," what processes can we put in place to ensure that every child has at least "one person in the whole world"? And how can we structure our educational systems so that school people are systematically accorded their due recognition and appreciation for the critical roles they play in our children's lives?

3. Wheaton College

What can you do to become even more effective when you are a seasoned, savvy university vice president and dean at an up-and-coming university, and your organization has ambitious plans?

Vision 2014: Wheaton College develops global citizens prepared to lead in a complex world. Its transformational learning environment prepares graduates to live purposeful lives, be engaged in their communities, be scientifically and technologically literate, and act effectively to promote change.

—Affirmed by the Board of Trustees on May 19, 2006

How do you position yourself and your organization when the July 30, 2006, *New York Times* writes of Wheaton that it is "singled out as a choice for students looking for a more intimate experience"? How do you prepare yourself when the October 29, 2006, issue of the weekly *Boston Globe Magazine* features your president on the cover with the headline, "Dr. Popularity: Wheaton College President Ronald A. Crutcher talks about running a red-hot school, ignoring SAT scores, and cello practice at dawn"? What do you do when it becomes general knowledge that this tiny university has cultivated three Rhodes scholars in the past 6 years?

Gail Berson, Wheaton's dean of admission and student financial services, recognized that Wheaton College was on the rise, and she was committed to preparing her staff for the challenges of the Strategic Plan and the impending changes. After considerable reflection (with me as her consultant), Berson decided to host a retreat in order to strengthen the communication within and between her two departments.

After gathering at Colonial Blackinton Inn for breakfast, the 30-plus members of the Admission and Student Financial Services team quickly proceeded with AI-inspired paired interviews between people who generally do not work together. Questions they covered during a half-hour interviewing session focused on working collaboratively and included the following:

• "As you reflect back on your years working at Wheaton College, either in your current role or in a previous role, focus on a high point when you accomplished much with another person or a group of people . . . and important results were achieved. Please tell me the story."

• "We each have different qualities and skills we bring to our work. . . . Without being humble, what do you most value about yourself that you bring to working with others? What are your best qualities, skills, values, approaches?"

• "Imagine that you are Rip Van Winkle, and you fell asleep for 3 years. When you wake up, it is November 28, 2009. Palpable shifts have happened, and your work situation in Admission and Financial Aid is a 'dream-come-true.' What would things be like overall? What three changes are making the biggest difference? What has shifted in you?"

After the paired conversations, each group of two people joined three other pairs and introduced their partners to the others at the table. The responses to the above questions allowed each person to become more widely known for his or her successes, values, and hopes. The entire division then had the opportunity to learn about the gifts of the total community and to uncover best practices and conditions that are conducive to a thriving organization.

Next, people who worked in somewhat similar roles formed "tribes" and articulated, "What is our tribe doing well? And what do I value about the contributions of other tribes in the Admission and Financial Aid community?" In the large group, the tribes bragged about their contributions and appreciated the specific contributions of those in other roles. Following this, the tribes identified what they were doing that they could do more often to be even more effective, as well as what they could do differently. They were also asked to identify what other tribes could do more often as well as consider doing differently. The final assignment was for each tribe to create a poem, a skit, a dance, or a song that reflected their hopes and possibilities.

Participants were enthusiastic about being known and about having the opportunity to share their insights about themselves and other groups in a safe environment.

Participants were enthusiastic about being known and about having the opportunity to share their insights about themselves and other groups in a safe environment. Several tribes amazed themselves and others with their creative songs, poems, and posters.

The feedback about this brief session was overwhelmingly positive. Overall, participants realized, "We are all on the same page!" Asked what was the most important aspect of the retreat, participants' statements included "Understanding of others' perspectives," "Finding out that everyone who attended seemed to have the same goals," "Being able to hear personal stories of triumphs as relayed by other staff members," "[Appreciating] openness to safely share opinions," "Being able to talk about my experience at Wheaton and to reflect in a positive way about my colleagues without recriminations," and "Opening lines of communication across divisions, positive and negative."

Asked what they learned that will help in day-to-day work, participants identified several important learnings: "Process before reaction"; "To look at the big picture and not get bogged down in the small details"; "Change is positive and we need to embrace it"; "To be more tolerant and positive"; "Positive attitude toward teamwork"; and "Remembering that we have a shared goal. Remembering everyone's good intentions." In response to a question about what could have made the retreat more useful, nearly all of the comments were about wishing that the retreat had been longer and that there had been opportunities to hear more stories.

Shortly after the staff retreat, Dean Berson commenced work to redesign the structure of the support operations in the Admission division. Continuing a high level of participation, the dean and a cross-functional Operations Committee planned a series of interventions that included (1) a group meeting with the counselors (those involved directly in recruiting students), (2) one-on-one interviews with each of the Operations staff members, (3) meetings with others who could bring an informed perspective to strengthening Operations, (4) a group meeting with the Operations staff, and (5) meetings between and among the Operations Committee, the dean, and the consultant.

In the spirit of AI, the process involved the 4-D cycle in all conversations: discovering life-giving forces, practices that are currently highly successful, and places where particular energy and talent reside. A subcommittee working with the consultant then crafted roles that will, according to the wisdom gleaned from the entire community, best serve as a platform to support Wheaton in achieving its mission.

As a consequence of the AI initiative, morale has improved, staff members feel connected to and invested in the outcomes, and a new appreciation for collaboration has emerged. Change is hard, and in any culture where ambiguity prevails over clarity, it is even harder. The process of Appreciative Inquiry has been at the heart of these changes; from the early victories that have come to pass, the dean, together with her staff in Admission and Student Financial Services, looks forward to a more effective and efficient office team.

4. College of Education, University of Memphis

The purpose of the Summit is to engage the faculty, students, staff, and community in creating the future direction of the College of Education. We have operated in silos; now we are building a choir with lots of voices singing from the same page.

—Ric Hovda, dean

How do you mobilize a traditional college of education to become a 21st-century leader in teacher development in a rapidly changing, interdependent world? It took Ric Hovda, dean of the College of Education at the University of Memphis, very little time to comprehend the power of inquiry and appreciation in enabling a new era. As he introduced his Core Planning Team to the use of this social technology, they could see no better way to move ahead than by engaging all stakeholders in achieving a "relevant, engaged, and leading" school of education. Beginning as a seed kernel, AI has now become institutionalized in Memphis; an annual summit engages large numbers of people from all relevant constituencies in systematically reexamining the college's progress toward becoming *the* leading metropolitan college of education.

In the fall of 2004, Dean Hovda assembled a core leadership team that was charged with transforming the College of Education. Beginning with 23 people who represented faculty, students, and staff, the group coalesced during a two-day Team Trek that focused on developing team competencies, including a draft of team norms. Through the dean's commitment of time and resources, the team was introduced to Appreciative Inquiry and was supported in designing and delivering a highly successful Futures Planning Summit, which started in 2005 and is now in its third year.

The expected outcomes of the Futures Planning Summit have included creating the future direction of the College of Education, clarifying the "positive core" of what was at the heart of the college's finest work, defining strategic action areas (termed "aspiration statements"), gaining ownership/buy-in for the plan's direction, and clarifying and igniting commitment from both internal and external stakeholders.

On May 9 and 10, 2005, in Memphis's beautiful Botanic Gardens, a collection of 240 diverse stakeholders gathered amid celebratory decorations, balloons, wall hangings, markers, crayons, and playthings. While participants had been informed that the College of Education hoped for their input and participation, a certain level of mystery and skepticism existed about what could actually be accomplished. Would there merely be a succession of talking heads? How could 2 days of meetings with such a large group yield anything worthwhile?

The planning team held its collective breath as, one by one, the university president, the chair of the Faculty Senate, students, faculty, and staff members started to show up. In addition, there were many representatives from organizations served by the college.

Preschool and public school practitioners of all kinds, ranging from teachers to superintendents, as well as representatives of government and youth organizations, had responded to the curiosity-provoking invitation.

As Mary Jo Greil, lead facilitator of the summit, guided the schedule, participants variously interacted in pairs, in small groups of eight at their tables, in special-interest teams, and with the entire group of 240 people. The clearly defined structure for the event provided emotional safety for the participants and reinforced the expectation for their active involvement throughout the 2-day summit. Three additional facilitators worked with the lead facilitator in supporting groups of 80 participants to make sure that they had access to needed resources and that they fully understood their tasks.

Throughout the summit, a graphics facilitator illustrated the emerging work that began to cover the ballroom walls. The illustrator's exceptional skill in capturing the presenters' intent in graphical form strongly supported the participants in their deliberations. His artistry mirrored and illuminated the essence of their strengths, hopes, challenges, and possible futures.

During the Discovery interviews and Dream presentations, each participant indicated his or her priorities for the various topic areas of the futures planning work of the college. Aspiration statements were developed by small groups and presented to the entire group for editing, revision, or (rarely) rejection. These distilled statements represented the strategic action areas—the "aspirations" of the College of Education over the next 3 years.

Through voting, the participants gave their overwhelming support to several statements, many of which aligned with the university's strategic areas of focus. These included statements about the recruitment, retention, and development of faculty, staff, and undergraduate and graduate students; program excellence through academic advising and mentoring; research and intellectual development; productive partnerships; Ph.D. programs; mutually beneficial clinical sites; and improved organizational structures and support systems. Participants joined the Innovation Implementation Team to which they were most attracted, drafting action steps, timelines, resources, and metrics for a 3-year period.

Comments about the summit were very positive. People realized that it was "easier to do planning as a result of having so many [constituencies] in that room, [after] listening to the very diverse opinions," than they had expected. One participant commented, "We started out with the babble of voices and progressed to voices that became clearer and ended up with priorities— everybody's voice was heard." One person observed, "Stakeholders were amazed that our college was opening up to that extent, taking voices seriously, [and there was] equity of voice compared to pre-summit silos."

"We started out with the babble of voices and progressed to voices that became clearer and ended up with priorities—everybody's voice was heard."

The summits of 2006 and 2007 have provided opportunities to build on the earlier work. At the 2006 summit, people from relevant constituencies again gathered to deepen their connections and to take stock of the progress of the College of Education. Each aspiration team presented its floor-to-ceiling laminated statement, then reported on its accomplishments over the past year. Building on that progress, each team crafted other concrete goals and activities that would advance the college toward the achievement of its vision. As the groups recommitted to the aspiration statements, there was a merging of the work from the summit with the conceptual framework that had begun prior to this effort with every department participating. The three commitment areas that surfaced were effective practice, commitment to diverse communities, and leadership.

Dean Hovda accepted the Core Team's recommended subtitle to the 2007 Summit III: *Decision Day.* In preparing for the summit, all of the aspiration teams are being asked to surface any "big ideas" in order for the college to sustain focus and help realize the guiding vision: "Create *the* Metropolitan College of Education that is engaged, relevant, and leading." As Dean Hovda said,

> The Summit is about the College and the synergy that occurs when faculty and staff commit time to have conversations about the future. The Summit is about community and renewing the spirit and commitments necessary to move forward. The Summit is about building connectedness. . . . gathering as a group to think together and to act together.

It may be helpful to reflect on questions such as these: What happens to the speed of deliberation and change when people who represent many different constituencies but share a common interest come together for a day or two? What happens when there is systemic engagement of all major constituencies, and what are the implications for transformational change? What kind of leadership qualities must be present? What are the other hypotheses that arise out of an experiment such as that undertaken by the University of Memphis College of Education?

5. AI Coaching for a Terminated Superintendent

Early one morning, I received a call from Patricia Ruane, superintendent of schools in the Lexington, Massachusetts, Public Schools—actually, *former* superintendent of schools. Within 3 minutes, she informed me that she had been fired by her school board the previous evening.

In many ways, Patricia had progressed through public school leadership roles in a typical fashion. She had been a classroom teacher, department head, principal, assistant superintendent, and superintendent in the Greater Boston area. She had served as the superintendent in Lexington for just under 2 years when she experienced the "sudden and surprising ending" of her superintendency with a "no-cause" dismissal.

My many years of using AI in coaching guided me in helping Pat to recover from what she described vividly as "a professional stroke." She observed, "People often lack the tools to pull the leader back to a state of full force and normal capacity." The one-on-one coaching process involved the 4-D cycle of Discovery, Dream, Design, and Destiny. Discovery questions seek strength, such as, "Everyone sooner or later runs into obstacles that are overwhelming and seem impossible to recover from. As you think back on your life experience, could you tell me a time when you overcame a tough situation where you not only met the challenge, but actually came out ahead?"

Or consider this classic Dream question (a variant of the one we used at Wheaton College): "Imagine that you are Rip Van Winkle, and you fell asleep for 3 years. When you wake up, it is now [a date 3 years in the future], and your work and personal life are exactly as you would like them to be. What would things be like overall? What three changes are making the biggest difference? What has shifted in you?"

Design questions, by inquiring what would need to happen in order for the dream to come true, build on the responses to Dream questions—for example, "You say that you want another job as a superintendent. What kinds of things do you feel you need to deal with from this past job in order to move forward?"

Finally, Destiny questions invite the person to take stock. In this case, the query might be, "So you are reconnecting with your former network. What are you learning about each person when you see or talk with them?" This phase allows for further calibration as experiments are evaluated and learnings are harvested.

In this coaching situation, Pat reconnected with and articulated her strengths, dreamed of what she longed for despite this horrendous setback, designed strategies and concrete actions she could take to recover her professional and personal self, and then arrived at her destiny of securing another role as superintendent. Her reflections are that the 4-D cycle "simultaneously pushed and affirmed me as a person and a professional, even as we did the hard work of going over painful territory in careful detail."

The use of Appreciative Inquiry in my professional coaching has consistently been a positive force in the work I do with clients. No matter what they are experiencing professionally or personally, I urge them to continually reflect on their assets, talents, knowledge, values, passions, and life-giving experiences. Grounded in the strengths that they know at the deepest level, they can harness this knowledge to provide the strength and confidence to deal with their present and to create the future, no matter how unfathomable it might seem. According to this recovered superintendent, AI coaching was "a light in the darkness."

POSTSCRIPT

6. KnowledgeWorks Foundation Educational Salon

What can interested parties do to get to the root of what it would take to create the conditions in which all schoolchildren can access an education that develops their fullest human capacity? What needs to be transformed, and what are the highest leverage interventions to bring those changes about? Learned faculty from schools of education, seasoned practitioners, church and civic leaders, worried parents, reflective authors, concerned philanthropists—all have voiced concern about the enormity of the challenge of educating all of our children. A multitude of experiments—some well known and some obscure, some generously funded and some not—have been and continue to be conducted. Amid myriad theories and calls for reform, KnowledgeWorks Foundation is beginning to host conversations that investigate these fundamental questions: "What is the purpose of education?" and "What are the core values we must live by in order to pursue our purpose most effectively?"

By sheer good fortune, three organizations of kindred spirit—the Center for Empowered Leadership, the Learning Circle, and KnowledgeWorks Foundation—came together to imagine what could begin a sea change in education. While the Educational Salon was not a "classic" Appreciative Inquiry gathering, two of the four conveners—Learning Circle founder Rita Cleary and this author—are grounded in AI. Thus, in the AI spirit of bringing representatives of all major constituencies together, we included key leaders from the American Association of School Administrators, the National Education Association, and the Harvard Medical School, as well as a variety of other leaders who have made a difference in the areas of social and emotional learning, gender, values, spirituality, and new models of teacher education.

The gathering was based on provocative questions, for which no known agreed-upon or easy answers exist. One participant suggested periods of silence throughout the salon, and this norm became a valued and important practice. People seemed particularly able to reflect as they listened deeply to themselves and to the varied voices in the room. Several of the questions

People move toward becoming the best version of themselves, enabling more conscious and creative strategy design and implementation. The AI process also helps people find meaning as they use their highest strengths in service to something larger than themselves.

elicited heartfelt stories, including comments about an imprisoned relative, the perspectives of children and grandchildren, and affectionate stories about favorite teachers and their life-changing impact. The spaciousness of the salon seemed to draw out elevated thinking that could have the power to inform wise action. The fundamental Appreciative Inquiry anticipatory principle was omnipresent—the recognition that the greatest resource for generating constructive organizational change is the emergence of the collective imagination through dialogue involving all stakeholders.

Daniel Kim's (2002) publication *Foresight as a Central Ethic of Leadership* served as a major reference throughout the salon, particularly a section about varying levels of perspective and accompanying action modes. In addition, KnowledgeWorks Foundation commissioned a Map of Future Forces Affecting Education, which served as a continuous reference for the group. "[KnowledgeWorks Foundation is] sharing this map with other catalysts for change in education because we hope it will also inspire them to take advantage of the possibilities opened by trends affecting families, communities, markets, institutions, educators, learning, tools, and practices" (KnowledgeWorks Foundation, 2006; see www.kwfdn.org/map).

The Educational Salon is very much a work in progress, and consideration is being given to how such a structure and a process can contribute to changing the color of the education ocean. From my several salon experiences, whether as a participant, convener, or facilitator, I have come to believe that gatherings based on Appreciative Inquiry principles—principles that many of us already hold—will help generate ways of bringing about the much-needed sea change in education. Through the valuing of all of the individual and collective voices in salon contexts, I have witnessed the emergence of collective wisdom, in which the whole is greater than the sum of the parts as a result of generative thinking together. Fields such as Appreciative Inquiry can make a contribution to our nation as it repurposes this potent enterprise.

REFLECTIONS

Just as plants turn toward the light, people too are heliotropes and turn toward light, positive energy, and appreciation. Through the use of capacity-building questions, Appreciative Inquiry helps clarify each person's signature strengths and what is working for him or her. This hopeful spirit is then infused throughout the entity—whether it is an individual, a team, an organization, a community, or a group of any size and interest. People move toward becoming the best version of themselves, enabling more conscious and creative strategy design and implementation. The AI process also helps people find meaning as they use their highest strengths in service to something larger than themselves.

The root of education is the Latin *educare*—to pull forth that which is deepest within us in order to develop mind, skill, knowledge, and character. Since AI stands out as the simplest yet most elegant method of pulling forth what lies within people, what better way to address the needs of education than through Appreciative

Inquiry? Our society can harvest some of the most valuable information and wisdom about the ways in which we can rejuvenate the institution of education if we pose profound questions to leaders, parents, children, teachers, and others. These insights that reside within us will provide the framework for new and better forms of education to emerge.

REFERENCES

Cooperrider, D. L., Stavros, J. M., & Whitney, D. K. (2003). *Appreciative inquiry handbook: The first in a series of AI workbooks for leaders of change.* San Francisco: Berrett-Koehler.

Kim, D. (2002). *Foresight as a central ethic of leadership.* Indianapolis, IN: Greenleaf Center for Servant Leadership.

KnowledgeWorks Foundation. (2006). *Map of future forces affecting education.* Retrieved on May 24, 2007, from http://www.kwfdn.org/map/background.aspx

Whitney, D. (1996, Winter). Postmodern principles and practices for large-scale organizational change and global cooperation. *Organizational Development Journal, 14*(4), 53–68.

CHAPTER FIVE

COMMUNITY IN SCHOOL

The Heart of the Matter

ERIC SCHAPS

Commercial enterprises that market their products to young people will go to extraordinary lengths to understand their target customers' tastes and reactions. They conduct questionnaire surveys and focus groups to gather all sorts of customer data. They ask cohorts of young people to record the times and places of product usage. They conduct field visits to youngsters' homes to document the contexts in which their product is used. American businesses realize the importance of tracking and understanding their customers. They know that their company's success, their bottom line, depends on this understanding. Whether it's Coca-Cola, Mattel, or Old Navy, knowing one's customers and their product experience is pivotal to every decision and every action.

What on earth, one might well ask, does this have to do with the soul of educational leadership? It is relevant because the leader's knowing students and their experience of schooling—knowing his or her "customers" and their experience of his or her "product"—is fundamental to effective leadership. It is just as important as the leader being fair, receptive, and forthcoming in dealing with students, parents, and staff. It is just as important as being knowledgeable and discerning about curriculum and instruction. It is just as important as maintaining a steady focus on student outcomes. Why? Because the leader's understanding of students' school experience is crucial for determining what's working and what isn't, for determining what priorities to set and how to realize them.

Students are entrusted to their school's care, and so its leaders are morally obliged to see that they are safe and supported.

There's something else, too. Students, being young, are highly impressionable and vulnerable. Because of this vulnerability, ensuring that their experience of school is positive is a moral as well as a pragmatic imperative. Students are entrusted to their school's care, and so its leaders are morally obliged to see that they are safe and supported. Here, "safety" refers to both physical and emotional safety, and "supportive" refers to students' feeling connected, valued, and respected. Supportiveness also refers to students' being able to find purpose and a reasonable measure of success in what they do—day after day, week after week, year after year.

An educational leader's reasons for attending closely to students' experience differ from those of the business executive. Profits—and the bonuses, stock options, and country club memberships that accompany them—aren't at issue. Rather, what's at stake is the leader's ability to bring critical information to bear to better serve the full range of students in his or her charge. By using this information to create a more supportive school, the leader helps to meet students' basic psychological needs—their need for a sense of belonging and connection to others; for autonomy ("voice and choice," in the vernacular); and for a sense of being a capable, worthy person; as well as their need for safety. When these needs are effectively met, students will "bond" to their school, in the same way an infant bonds to a mother who provides for it capably. They will become affectively committed to the school's goals and values, and they will strive to fit in and succeed. In this way, a virtuous circle is created in which happier and more motivated students join with staff to create an even more supportive and engaging school environment.

A substantial body of research confirms the importance of building a safe and supportive school environment. Much of this evidence comes from studies showing the benefits of building "connectedness" or a sense of "community in school"—students' experience of having positive relationships and being valued, respected, influential members of the classroom and school at large. Strengthening students' sense of community in school produces a wide range of desirable effects, including increased academic motivation, social understanding and competence, altruistic inclinations, appropriate conduct in school, and trust and respect for teachers (Osterman, 2000). It also helps to prevent alcohol and marijuana use, violent behavior, and other high-risk activities (Battistich, Schaps, Watson, Solomon, & Lewis, 2000; Blum, McNeely, & Rinehart, 2002). And over time, it improves academic achievement as measured by grades or test scores (Blum et al., 2002; Marshall & Caldwell, 2007), especially when coupled with academic press (i.e., high expectations and strong norms for student achievement) (Schaps, Battistich, & Solomon, 2004).

WHAT IS COMMUNITY IN SCHOOL?

What is it like to be part of a "caring school community"? It is being a valued, contributing member of a group dedicated to the shared purposes of helping and supporting all members as they work together, learn, and grow. At the heart of a high-community school are *respectful, supportive relationships among and between students, teachers, and parents.* We tend to learn best from, and with, those to whom we relate well. Supportive relationships enable children from diverse backgrounds to bring their personal experiences into the classroom comfortably and thereby to discover their common humanity. Supportive relationships among educators help them deal with the risks and stresses of changing professional practice. Supportive relationships help parents, especially those who otherwise would feel ill at ease, to take active roles in the school and in their children's education.

Emphasizing common purposes and ideals is also important for creating a sense of community. High-community schools deliberately emphasize not only the importance of learning, but also the other qualities that are essential to our society: fairness, concern for others, and responsibility. Doing so promotes shared commitment to the school's (and society's) goals, establishes common ground, and shapes the norms that govern daily interaction. Helping students to think about these ideals in relation to their daily life helps them to develop a deeper understanding of those ideals and the myriad ways in which they can be applied.

Regular *opportunities to help and collaborate with others* is a third feature of high-community schools. With frequent opportunities for helping and collaboration, and frequent opportunities to reflect on their interactions with others, students learn the skills of working with others and develop wider and richer networks of interpersonal relationships. Moreover, students experience the many satisfactions of contributing to the welfare of others.

Finally, high-community schools provide frequent *opportunities for autonomy and influence.* Having some choice in how one goes about one's own learning, and having some say in determining the norms and values that govern one's group and the decisions that affect it, are intrinsically rewarding and affirming for children as well as adults. The experience of autonomy and influence thus strengthens the individual's bonds to the community. It also helps to prepare the student for the demanding role of citizen in a democracy.

DISINTEREST IN COMMUNITY BUILDING REMAINS THE NORM

The mission statements of many schools set lofty goals pertaining to safety and supportiveness, and yet it is the rare administrator who tracks students' experience of school. Few administrators systematically survey or interview their students about that experience. Few ask their students about how things could be improved. Rarely does one undertake shadowing students as they move through the school day. Among the few leaders who do collect some form of experiential information from students, fewer still disaggregate the data to discover, for example, whether African Americans feel as safe or engaged as Anglo students—despite definitive research showing that low-income students and students of color experience less connectedness than their affluent and Caucasian counterparts (Battistich, Solomon, Kim, Watson, & Schaps, 1995).

High-community schools deliberately emphasize not only the importance of learning, but also the other qualities that are essential to our society: fairness, concern for others, and responsibility.

Why this disinterest? Perhaps it is because the information could be unsettling. It certainly would be unsettling to an administrator to learn that being at school is less than a happy experience for a substantial proportion of students, or that it is downright aversive for a goodly number.

Another reason might be that students are much more of a captive audience than Pepsi drinkers or iPod users. Knowing that most students lack viable alternatives to attending their current school, it's fairly easy to treat their levels of enjoyment and satisfaction as secondary issues.

It's also possible, perhaps probable, that many leaders lack interest because they are running flat out to respond to the other demands on them. Never before have educators been asked to do so much for so many. They are required to deal with a student population that is the largest, most diverse, most needy, and most precocious but least socialized in the nation's history. They are required to help these students stay in school longer and achieve at higher academic levels—much higher levels—than ever before. They are required to rear as well as educate these students—to help them avoid drug use; delay sexual gratification; learn manners and social skills; and become civic minded, principled, and caring. And, should they ever fail to make "adequate yearly progress," they are likely to be branded as unmotivated or inept.

District and school administrators could easily be so overextended that suggesting they add one more thing to their plates, even something they know to be beneficial, would elicit an angry or even cynical response such as, "Are you kidding?! I'm maxed out already. Forget about it!" But suggesting one more thing—working assiduously to build all students' sense of community—is precisely the thrust of this chapter. The benefits are so wide-ranging, long-term, and substantial, and the necessary investments are sufficiently modest, that community building is truly a no-brainer. As an educational priority, it ought to rank right up there with maintaining high expectations for all students' learning, or for creating challenging and engaging learning opportunities for all students. It can go a long way toward accomplishing what a complex menu of discrete "affective education" programs—e.g., character education, social and emotional learning, drug prevention, violence prevention—is often cobbled together to do. Because it accomplishes multiple objectives, a serious focus on community building can actually simplify life for an administrator.

METHODS OF BUILDING COMMUNITY IN SCHOOL

One way to make it easier for administrators to take on the challenge of strengthening community in school is by equipping them with feasible methods for doing so. Fortunately, a lot has been learned in the past 20 years about what works in the classroom, in the school at large, and in linking home and school. Proven, affordable ways of building community have been developed and shown to be effective across a wide variety of school settings (Schaps et al., 2004). Approaches that have been shown to yield good results include the following:

- Class meetings in which students, with the teacher's help, have opportunities to set class goals and ground rules, to plan activities, to assess their progress, and to solve common problems. Class meetings give students a forum in which they can get to know one another, discuss issues, and make decisions that affect classroom climate.

- Cooperative learning groups in which students collaborate on academic tasks and have regular opportunities to plan and reflect on the ways they work together. These can involve the learning of social as well as academic skills, so that young children practice taking turns or showing that they are listening, while older students practice ways to build on each other's ideas or disagree respectfully.

- "Buddy" programs that regularly bring together whole classes of younger and older students to work one-on-one on academic, service, and recreational activities. Buddy programs help to build caring cross-age relationships and create a schoolwide climate of trust.

- Inclusive whole-school events involving students and their families in ways that capitalize on their diverse backgrounds and personal experiences, such as "Family Heritage Week" or a "family hobbies fair." These activities link students, parents, and school staff in building a caring school environment They also foster new school traditions and promote involvement of parents who typically do not participate at school.

- Service learning opportunities inside and outside the school that enable students to contribute to the welfare of others and to reflect on their experiences while doing so. These can range from simple school beautification and clean-up projects to community organizing campaigns that have ambitious civic goals. In every case, however, the initiative involves true collaboration and is coupled with deliberate needs assessment, planning, and reflection activities that clarify and solidify students' learning.

Because it accomplishes multiple objectives, a serious focus on community building can actually simplify life for an administrator.

When implemented properly, these community-building approaches become an integral part of a school's overall improvement efforts. They become seamlessly woven into the school's policies, pedagogies, and daily routines. They are *not* regarded as add-ons, as in "Now it's time to focus on building community."

MEASURING COMMUNITY IN SCHOOL

Measuring a sense of community in school is relatively straightforward, beginning in fourth or possibly third grade. Typically it is done by surveying students with a brief questionnaire once during the year. (Administering the survey at the same time each year is advisable if one wants to chart progress over time, since responses seem to vary with time of year.)

In the pioneering "National Adolescent Longitudinal Health Study" conducted in the 1990s, principal investigator Robert Blum and colleagues (Blum et al., 2002; Resnick et al., 1997) used a simple five-item scale to measure what they term school connectedness. They asked a national sample of 12,000 students in Grades 7 through 12, "How strongly do you agree or disagree with each of the following statements?":

- I feel close to people at this school.
- I am happy to be at this school.
- I feel like I am part of this school.
- The teachers at this school treat students fairly.
- I feel safe in my school.

Respondents answered on a five-point continuum from *strongly agree* to *strongly disagree*. The scale was shown to predict students' resistance to a variety of problem behaviors including alcohol, tobacco, and marijuana use; violence; emotional distress and suicidal thoughts; and early sexual behavior. The scale also predicted students' grades in major academic subjects. Perhaps more than any other study, the "Add Health Study," as it is often called, has demonstrated the importance of community in school for students' academic success and their avoidance of high-risk behavior.

My organization, the Developmental Studies Center (DSC), has measured elementary students' sense of community in school in a series of major evaluation studies beginning in the 1980s and continuing through the 1990s, involving a sizable number of urban, suburban, and rural districts scattered around the United States. We used a three-part scale for this purpose. One subscale we used, called Classroom Supportiveness, consists of 14 items, including

- My class is like a family.
- Students in my class help each other learn.
- Students in my class treat each other with respect.
- Students in my class work together to solve problems.

Similar to the Blum study, students indicate the degree to which they agree or disagree with each item along a five-point continuum. A second subscale, Autonomy and Influence in the Classroom, includes 10 items such as

- In my class, students have a say in what goes on.
- In my class, the teacher and students plan together what we will do.
- Students in my class can get a rule changed if they think it is unfair.
- My teacher lets me choose what I will work on.

The third and last subscale, School Supportiveness, consists of 14 items, including

- Students at this school really care about each other.
- I feel I can talk with teachers at this school about things that are bothering me.

- Students at this school are willing to go out of their way to help someone.
- Teachers and students treat each other with respect at this school.

One of the major findings from DSC's studies is that building a sense of community during the elementary school years yields benefits that last at least through middle school. During middle school, students from high-community elementary schools scored higher than those from other schools with respect to various school-related attitudes and behaviors (e.g., trust in teachers, liking for school, engagement in class activities), and they achieved higher grade-point averages and better scores on district tests. They also continued to manifest more prosocial attitudes and behaviors (Battistich, Schaps, & Wilson, 2004).

By the way, DSC allows educators and researchers to use our "sense of community" scale at no cost. We do so because we believe so strongly in the importance of measuring community on an annual basis. The scale can be found on our Web site: www.devstu.org. (We do ask that those wishing to use it write for permission to do so, and that they share with us, if possible, the data they collect so that over time we can build a national database.)

Building a sense of community during the elementary school years yields benefits that last at least through middle school.

CONDITIONS FOR SUCCESSFUL COMMUNITY BUILDING

We at DSC have worked with many districts around the country over the past 26 years. In the process, we have learned that efforts to build caring, inclusive, participatory school environments tend to succeed under certain conditions and to flounder under others. From the outset, our mission has been to support public schools that seek to help children develop to their fullest potential ethically, socially, and emotionally as well as academically. Our programs are designed to make the climate of the classroom and school more supportive and to reshape literacy and math instruction in ways that foster affective as well as cognitive growth.

We have worked with a wide range of school systems: large and small; urban, suburban, and rural; wealthy and poor; diverse and homogeneous. We frequently have worked with district leaders, over a period of several years, to help them introduce our programs and to develop their internal capacity to foster high-quality program implementation. Thanks to more than $75 million in grant funding from 45 philanthropic and governmental sources—much of it designated for demonstration studies that incorporated rigorous process and outcome evaluation—we have been able to track the effects of our efforts on how classrooms and schools actually function, as well as on student outcomes. Below are five lessons we have learned about the conditions and influences that facilitate or impede the effective adoption of holistic programs in general, and community-building programs in particular.

1. District and school leaders must actively lead community-building efforts if they are to be successful. It should come as no surprise that parents and teachers want their schools to be safe and happy places for students. We have found that the vast majority of teachers, especially at the elementary level, feel just as parents do about a nurturing environment. Teachers, too, want their students to look forward to coming to school, to develop a love of learning, and to acquire the values, sensibilities, and competencies that will enable them eventually to fulfill their adult roles not just as workers but also as citizens, spouses, parents, and so forth.

But this grassroots affinity for community building and for educating the "whole child" does not matter much when, as is often the case, a district's leadership is not also strongly committed. The district office is so important because instructional and curricular decisions increasingly are made there, whereas even a few years ago such decisions often were made within the individual school. Moreover, individual schools often lack the expertise to find, and the resources to pay for, effective programs. So schools are increasingly subject to district-level demands and influences and are in great need of district assistance to obtain effective support for ambitious change efforts. It's critical, therefore, that district leaders be knowledgeable about community building and that they marshal resources and personnel to assist in the change process. Unless community building is a genuine district- as well as school-level priority, it is unlikely to happen with quality, depth, consistency, and longevity.

It's often said that the principal is key to successful change within a school. We strongly concur. In fact, we have *never* seen a school faculty succeed at pulling off an ambitious change effort, even when it had the enthusiastic support of the school's parent group, by end-running around a principal who had a different set of priorities in mind. Principals simply have too much formal and informal influence, and control too many resources, to be on the sidelines of, let alone be working against, an ambitious effort to build community in a school. Unless the principal champions an ambitious change effort, it just won't happen.

2. Most classroom teachers need curricular and instructional materials that are designed to help them become proficient and comfortable with community building. Two decades ago, John Goodlad (1984) found that most classroom instruction in this country was didactic, with students kept in very passive roles throughout the school day. Our experience suggests that Goodlad's findings still apply: Most classroom teachers do not—and do not know how to—create inclusive, participatory, caring classroom communities. Most do not use cooperative learning methods, class meetings, or partnering work as a matter of routine. Most do not know how to create academic tasks that are better done collaboratively than individually. When they do create such tasks, they often do not prepare their students to work together effectively. And most do not know how to engage students in thoughtful reflection on what has been experienced and learned, academically, ethically, or socially.

We have also learned the hard way that only a small proportion of classroom teachers—perhaps 10% to 20%—can effectively reinvent their own instructional practice from an overarching set of principles or concepts. This percentage may be even smaller when teachers are first learning those concepts and principles. The vast majority of teachers need concrete, sequenced instructional materials that respond to their common, legitimate question: "Okay, I like this approach, but exactly what should I do Monday morning? And then what do I do on Tuesday?" These teachers need instructional materials that, over time, systematically scaffold their learning of new principles and methods. It is important to differentiate such staged and structured guidance—which allows teachers the latitude to choose among or adapt the suggested practices and activities—from fully "scripted" programs that ignore or override teachers' professional judgment. Fully scripted programs are unlikely to promote the judgment and skill that teachers must develop over time for holistic instruction and classroom management.

3. Most educators need more professional development than is usually provided to effect change. The common wisdom, with which we wholeheartedly agree, is that simply providing good instructional materials is insufficient for most teachers to alter classroom practice in meaningful ways. Because community building requires that teachers learn how to attend and respond to a broad range of considerations, many of them need ongoing support in order to become comfortable and proficient. We believe that the *combination* of high-quality instructional materials with professional development is necessary for a wide range of teachers to succeed at community building. Often it takes a full year of support for a broad range of teachers in a typical public school to successfully incorporate class meetings and cooperative learning approaches into their pedagogy. During that time, they may need to be protected from competing demands for major change—so that they are not being asked, for example, to revamp their math program at the same time. They are likely to need regular opportunities to meet as a whole faculty to discuss professional issues related to the desired changes; to meet in small groups to plan their lessons together, observe each other, and debrief; and for follow-up skill-building workshops, preferably conducted by practitioners who have already mastered the new approach.

We believe that the combination of high-quality instructional materials with professional development is necessary for a wide range of teachers to succeed at community building.

Unfortunately, over the past decade, the amount of time available for professional development in most districts has decreased significantly. There are various reasons for this, but common ones include shortages of substitute teachers, contract limits on the number and length of faculty meetings, and, most important, very limited staff development budgets. Districts and schools do not budget anywhere near what many other kinds of organizations spend on improving their workforce.

On the positive side, we recently have seen a trend in medium-sized and large districts toward building an internal, district-level cadre of full-time staff developers who work directly with teachers (and sometimes principals) to support improvements in classroom practice. When such internal staff developers possess real expertise, and are actually deployed to work with teachers in an ongoing way, they can provide very effective support.

4. High-stakes, test-based, short-term accountability systems can be a formidable obstacle to building community. With some notable exceptions, as we have worked closely with district leaders and have gained the access and trust that enable us to watch the high-level decision making that occurs in the central office, we have seen the need to "beat the test" swamp other priorities—if not immediately, then within a few years, as the bar that defines academic success gets raised higher and higher. We have seen the same thing happen with principals' decision making at the school level. As long as performance is judged primarily or solely on the basis of achievement test scores, as is the case with current federal and state accountability systems, it takes an exceptionally strong-minded, well-established superintendent or principal to see that community-building goals and priorities are not marginalized. The toll on those exceptional leaders can be great as they personally serve as buffers against the prevailing pressures; many begin to wilt as the pressures mount, and many reluctantly resort to such "beat the test" strategies as allocating more time and resources for test prep or reducing instructional time in untested subject areas (e.g., social studies, music, art).

We have also witnessed mounting frustration and anger among classroom teachers as pressure on them has increased to produce gains in test scores. This anger stems in part from their belief that standardized tests do not measure what is most important academically. Also in part it comes from their sense that it is unrealistic and unfair to expect schools alone to eliminate the so-called achievement gap. In addition, a good deal of their anger comes from feeling that they can no longer pursue the holistic reasons they had for entering teaching. Some of the very best classroom teachers we have encountered have left the profession, often retiring 5 or 10 years earlier than they had planned, rather than alter their practice to comply with the new testing imperative. All of this, of course, compounds the difficulty of community building.

5. School goals, policies, and procedures must be community-friendly. A school's practices and procedures can easily undermine community. For example, many schools honor only their most

academically and athletically gifted students. Administrators can enhance community by seeing to it that accomplishments and contributions of many kinds are honored. Discipline policies must be sufficiently robust to ensure order and safety but must not be so exacting or punitive that they cause anger and alienation. The schools' limited resources must be judiciously allocated so that perceptions of privilege do not arise. The need to cover the whole curriculum adequately—which has become a daunting challenge, given the proliferation of demanding, comprehensive academic standards in every subject area—must be moderated by the need for students to be active, interactive, and reflective in the learning process. None of this is easy. All of it constitutes a constant balancing act—one that can be enhanced by involving students themselves in the process of needs assessment and problem solving.

CONCLUSION

To sum up, schools must engage and inspire students' hearts as well as their minds, and this requires that schools get better at meeting students' basic, legitimate needs—their needs for safety, belonging, competence, and autonomy. In other words, students will care about a school's goals and values when that school effectively cares for them. The best schools are those that enlist students as active, influential participants in creating a caring and just environment in the classroom and in the school at large. The challenge is for the school to become a microcosm in which students practice age-appropriate versions of the roles—and face the related challenges—they must face in later life. The goal is a total school culture in which all stakeholders, including administrators, teachers, and support staff as well as students and parents, treat one another with kindness and respect.

REFERENCES

Battistich, V., Schaps, E., Watson, M., Solomon, D., & Lewis, C. (2000). Effects of the Child Development Project on students' drug use and other problem behaviors. *Journal of Primary Prevention, 21,* 75–99.

Battistich, V., Schaps, E., & Wilson, N. (2004). Effects of an elementary school intervention on students' "connectedness" to school and social adjustment during middle school. *Journal of Primary Prevention, 24,* 243–262.

Battistich, V., Solomon, D., Kim, D., Watson, M., & Schaps, E. (1995). Schools as communities, poverty levels of student populations, and students' attitudes, motives, and performance: A multilevel analysis. *American Educational Research Journal, 32,* 627–658.

Blum, R. W., McNeely, C. A., & Rinehart, P. M. (2002). *Improving the odds: The untapped power of schools to improve the health of teens.* Minneapolis: Center for Adolescent Health and Development, University of Minnesota.

Goodlad, J. (1984). *A place called school: Prospects for the future.* New York: McGraw Hill.

Marshall, J., & Caldwell, S. (2007). Caring school community the Character*plus* way. In *The Character*plus* Way Results Monograph.* St. Louis, MO: Cooperating School Districts, 13–20.

Osterman, K. (2000). Students' need for belonging in school. *Review of Educational Research, 70*(3), 323–367.

Resnick, M. D., Bearman, P. S., Blum, R. W., Bauman, K. E., Harris, K. M., Jones, J., et al. (1997). Protecting adolescents from harm: Findings from the National Longitudinal Study on Adolescent Health. *Journal of the American Medical Association, 278*(10), 823–832.

Schaps, E., Battistich, V., & Solomon, D. (2004). Community in school as key to student growth: Findings from the Child Development Project. In J. Zins, R. Weissberg, M. Wang, & H. Walberg (Eds.), *Building academic success on social and emotional learning: What does the research say?* (pp. 189–205). New York: Teachers College Press.

CHAPTER SIX

THE STORIES OF PRACTICING SUPERINTENDENTS

The Struggle to Make the Right Decisions

CLAIRE SHEFF KOHN

Recounting narratives of experience has been the major way throughout recorded history that humans have made sense of their experience.

—I. E. Seidman (1991)

SETTING THE SCENE

I was a new superintendent—brand new, with only a month on the job—when I was faced with the daunting task of cutting the district's budget by 15% after three ballot attempts to get the needed funds had been rejected by the voters. How was I going to decide what to cut? In the end, I was the one who had to weigh the disparate input and decide what cuts to recommend. And in the end, I based my recommendations on my own values about education and what I believed to be "right," knowing my recommendations would affect the education of students and the lives of employees and their families.

In another district where I served as superintendent, I received a call one day from one of my principals. He said, "Claire, are you sitting down?" When I assured him I was, he announced, "One of our teachers has discovered a video camera under a table in the women's bathroom. It was taping through a hole in the tablecloth." We soon had evidence that another teacher in the building, a male, likely was responsible for the videotaping. What was I to do? Suspend the suspected culprit with pay, pending further investigation? Allow him to report to work until we knew for sure? Weighing my concern for the safety and well-being of the staff and students against the interests of this individual, I made the decision to suspend him and bar him from the premises. Although many of the decisions associated with this case were somewhat cut and dried, it didn't make the experience any easier. After all, I was the instrument by which his life and career would be changed irrevocably.

In the end, I was the one who had to weigh the disparate input and decide what cuts to recommend. And in the end, I based my recommendations on my own values about education and what I believed to be "right."

In that same district, I was confronted with a teacher strike. The union voted to authorize their leadership to call a strike, which they did on the teachers' first day back to school. They threatened to stay out the next day, too, which was the students' first day back, if an agreement were not reached. I had to decide whether or not to implement our strike plan and open school with administrators, support staff, substitutes, and volunteers. But how was I to make that determination? After considering the choices, I decided to open school, basing my decision on what I believed to be the best for the students and the district and what I thought was the right thing to do.

How to Know What's Right

As a school superintendent, I make decisions that affect people's lives and livelihoods. In making those decisions, I struggle to do my best to determine what's right and to act accordingly. But how do I know what's right? I have been a superintendent for almost 19 years now. I have served in four districts, in two states. In each job, I have been

confronted with difficult decisions associated with budgets, personnel, labor negotiations, students, school boards, parents, safety and
security, and every other aspect of the superintendency. You'd think it
would get easier, but it doesn't. Experience certainly helps, but I still
wrestle with difficult decisions.

Throughout my career, I have tried to gather "wisdom" wherever
I can—from professional development opportunities, reading materials, and my colleagues. Along the way, I attended the Ethical
Fitness Seminar sponsored by the Institute for Global Ethics. I had
one of those "Eureka!" moments when Rush Kidder, the institute's
founder, talked about the most difficult moral dilemmas as those
involving "right versus right," not those involving "right versus
wrong." He helped me understand that the really mind-bending,
spirit-testing decisions are those with more than one right answer,
and those in which competing values are represented. Such dilemmas certainly have been the most challenging and troublesome for
me! For example, should I make decisions based on what's right for
the student? The teachers? Parents? Taxpayers? Should I decide
based on a certain principle such as accountability for one's actions?
Compassion for the individual? Concern for the common good?
Adherence to policies or contracts?

My first story above shows
me now that I struggled mightily
with the decisions about what to
cut because multiple values that
I hold dear were in conflict. I didn't
want to cut anything, and yet I had
to present arguments defending
some choices over others, which
I based on a "hierarchy of values,"

*Rush Kidder helped me understand
that the really mind-bending,
spirit-testing decisions are those
with more than one right answer,
and those in which competing
values are represented.*

thereby ranking core subjects and the arts above cocurricular
offerings.

In the second example, it bothered me deeply to have to hurt
another human being and his innocent family. At the same time, he
had committed a crime and had violated the privacy and trust of his
colleagues, school, and district.

In the third example, the striking teachers, again I experienced
the conflict of competing values. I wanted to maintain good relations
with an employee group, yet to do so would mean violating higher
values associated with the education of students and the responsible
operation of the district.

The Ethical Fitness Seminar provided me with a means for thinking about my values and decision-making process. I can't say that my decisions have become any easier for having gained this new way of thinking, but I now have a way of reflecting on decisions and actions, either before or after, that makes sense to me. That helps.

HOW YOU MAKE DECISIONS IS "WHO YOU ARE"

I also learned something valuable about superintendents and their decision-making processes (my own included) when I wrote my doctoral dissertation, *Exploratory Case Study of the Power Problem of the Superintendency.* I developed my own theory about the effective use of power by superintendents through an ethnographic study of four sitting superintendents considered by state-level leaders of various education-related organizations to be successful in the exercise of power in moving their districts forward. The following universal themes I identified in the four case studies are relevant to a discussion of spirituality and decision making:

- Leadership in the superintendency is values-based.
- Superintendents experience a sense of isolation and loneliness on the job.
- Superintendents share a strong work ethic that springs from similar socioeconomic backgrounds.

As one of the participants in my study put it, "Where you take your organization is who you are" (Sheff Kohn, 1995, p. 311). That being the case, wouldn't the same be true of decision making—that your decisions are based on "who you are"? I decided I needed to confirm this belief by again talking to sitting superintendents. My primary goal was to gather superintendents' stories about spirituality, particularly as it relates to their decision making and to associated actions on the job. I asked them not only for their thoughts but also for specific examples from their practice because I wanted the discussion to be concrete and contextual.

HOW WERE THE CONVERSATIONS ORGANIZED?

I contacted 10 colleagues in Massachusetts and New Jersey, telling them that I had been asked to write a chapter for a book about spirituality in educational leadership and asking for their thoughts on the subject. All but one agreed to have a conversation with me. The participants included six women and three men, representing a range of experience as superintendents from 2 years to well over 20. They all had the same initial reaction: "I don't think I have much to offer of any value, but I'm willing to talk to you about it."

I arranged a date and time to meet with each superintendent. All but two of the interviews were done over the phone. One interview was done face-to-face, and one was done initially in person, with the remainder completed over the phone. The interviews lasted anywhere from an hour and fifteen minutes to two hours and thirty minutes. To give the superintendents some idea of what I hoped to cover and a chance to think about the topic in advance of our discussion if they wanted to, I sent them some guiding topics by e-mail. I started with the topic of what motivates them to be superintendents and a more general discussion about values as a way to establish rapport and as a "warm-up" of sorts before tackling more personal questions about religion and spirituality. I did not audiotape the interviews; I took notes on a form I devised for this purpose. I explained to the participating superintendents that I would be taking notes, and I read back selected comments to them to be sure I had captured what they intended and asked follow-up questions when I wasn't clear about what they meant. I told them I would not identify them or their districts, which I believe allowed them to be as candid as they were.

After completing the nine interviews, I organized the superintendents' remarks by topic, including the following:

1. What motivates them to be superintendents;

2. What gets them through difficult times at work;

3. Examples of difficult decisions they have had to make and whether or not they had to compromise their values in making these decisions;

4. What guides their decision making;

5. Where they believe their values came from;

6. Their views regarding the differences between being "religious" and being "spiritual"; and

7. The role of religion and/or spirituality in their decision making and related actions on the job.

I then established thematic connections among the experiences of the interviewees using these seven topics. In the following pages, I will share the superintendents' stories, using their exact words, in order to demonstrate the themes I found arising from the interviews.

What Motivates Superintendents to Do What They Do for a Living?

There was considerable agreement among all nine superintendents as to why they do what they do for a living and what gives them meaning and purpose. Four main themes emerged from my conversations with them; the quotes I have selected represent the thinking of the majority.

All the respondents expressed, in one way or another, that they are in their positions first and foremost for students. This theme was universal.

All the respondents expressed, in one way or another, that they are in their positions first and foremost for students. This theme was universal. As one superintendent put it, "Kids come first. All decisions need to be based on what's good for kids." Another summed it up by saying, "We work *with* people *for* kids." A third said, "I help adults and children to fulfill their potential. I now do that more with adults, but it's *for* students." And another commented, "I entered the profession because I wanted to help people—teachers; parents; support staff; and, of course, the kids."

Tied to their first priority of serving students was the second theme of working with and through others, particularly administrators, to change culture, to improve instruction, and to make education better. One superintendent remarked, "I like building good working relationships with professionals to get things done, and putting ideas into action by working with others to shape reality—from research into action." Another superintendent told me, "Problem solving and analyzing situations [with other district administrators] move us forward with something better than what we have." Yet another said, "I choose personnel who share my vision and values, which has helped us change the culture from one of disrespect to one of restored civility and trust." A fourth superintendent talked about her "belief in the power of people working together" and that she is "good at getting people committed and getting their support." She concluded, "I adore working with my small group of administrators and watching the ideas pop."

The notion of leaving a legacy was a third theme that emerged from the conversations. One superintendent captured this theme rather well when he told me,

> The opportunity to make a difference in the lives of children and adults through education has been consistent all along in my career. In a larger perspective, I have sought to help young people develop so they can be active, participating members of society because they will have the knowledge, skills, values, and perspective they need to do that. The importance for society is that education is power, and you can make a difference with it. Moving out of the classroom to a leadership position was an opportunity to have an impact over multiple years rather than only one year, one class at a time. You can see growth over time.

Another superintendent remarked, "I get a sense of accomplishment, an internal feeling. . . . I have a frame of reference spanning grades K–12 over 13 years in the district. I didn't begin thinking about this, but now I reflect on the impact I have had on kids' education." A third said, "I see more engaged kids, which means I have made a difference. That gives me satisfaction." And another commented, "You affect people you don't even know. You don't do it for the money or to get positive feedback that may never come or not until years later. You're happy you did it with or without confirmation."

As one put it simply, "As superintendent, you can make things happen."

A fourth theme that emerged from the interviews was that of preparing the "next generation" of educational leaders. One superintendent talked about "recruiting and mentoring new administrators to make schools better so kids can succeed, and improve instruction toward the same end," while another commented, "As my career advanced, I felt the need to groom the next generation of leaders, nudging people to reach, to develop courage to do things

When the going gets tough, the superintendents I interviewed described a variety of means—primarily through other people including family and friends, colleagues, and fellow superintendents—to find relief during difficult times.

they might not otherwise have done." A third said, "I help adults [in the district] to learn to think things through, and I model respect and responsibility. I empower them. I help them to be good people."

What Gets Superintendents Through the Difficult Times?

When the going gets tough, the superintendents I interviewed described a variety of means—primarily through other people including family and friends, colleagues, and fellow superintendents—to find relief during difficult times. As Roland Barth (2003) stated in *Lessons Learned: Shaping Relationships and the Culture of the Workplace,* "Very little in our lives is more important and more pervasive than our relationships with those we care about and with whom we work" (p. xi).

It's interesting to note that this was the only place where there were differences between the responses of the male and female superintendents, with the women mentioning family and friends while the men did not. It's not that the men don't have families and friends and enjoy their support; I know for a fact that they do. It's just that they didn't specifically identify them as a source of support, as the women did.

There was also a difference between those female superintendents with families at home as compared to those without anyone at home. As one superintendent observed, "There are no distractions for those of us without partners, children, and grandchildren. It creates an imbalance; it's all-consuming, and you don't notice it until you experience something else." In her case, she said, "I visit schools. I force myself out [of the office] to see kids and visit classrooms when I am having a bad day."

A typical reaction to the question about getting through the difficult times at work came from one female superintendent who said, "Getting involved in something else—the dog waiting at the door, my husband and son—they are there in good times and bad." Another superintendent offered, "Certainly family, because that's what matters most: family and friends. Those who come to board meetings are not personal." She went on to talk about the "people who have helped me and supported me selflessly and provided important perspectives," and "the people who 'sneak in' to tell me I have done a good job." A third superintendent pointed to her husband whom she credited with "always being there," and her parents, too. A fourth observed, "People make the difference, good people who provide support and who 'have your back.'" And a fifth said, "I unload and get advice from fellow superintendents." The one male superintendent who mentioned people as a support reported, "I am surrounded by people I can talk to who understand and help me to understand how to fix it, even telling me to stop whining and get off my ass and fix it."

As noted above, the most common answer for dealing with the pressure and stress among the superintendents, particularly the females, had to do with other people providing support and advice. In addition, some sought solace through other means, such as exercise, reflection on the past, or looking inside to find strength. One superintendent said, "When I face really tough times, I have to get out of here. I need other anchors to calm me down. I work out at a 'Y,' cycle, and get physical exercise." Another said, "I'm reflective. I look back at good things. I'm a glass-half-full kind of person. I remember the accomplishments." Similarly, another superintendent remarked, "I tap into instances of proof of my impact and legacy. I celebrate the successes. Seeing the legacy in the kids I have taught—I hang onto some of these things because I don't get much positive feedback. And yet it's what drives us." Still another said, "I have a strong belief in myself. I have integrity and good moral character. I have moments of doubt, but I know what's true. I try to make decisions for the right reasons and for the kids who are my responsibility."

None of the superintendents said they turn to religion, though one remarked, "I'm not religious, but at night I thank God for things." Another mentioned, "Some people turn to religion. I'm religious, but I don't turn to religion at such times." And another superintendent said, "It felt good in [community name] to be able to say 'I'm praying for you.' It's accepted there, but not elsewhere."

And one superintendent jokingly asked, "Oh, did I mention Scotch?"

WHAT DIFFICULT DECISIONS DO SUPERINTENDENTS MAKE, AND DO THEY EVER COMPROMISE THEIR BASIC VALUES WHEN MAKING THEM?

Asked to provide examples of the difficult decisions they have to make, the superintendents identified three main categories:

- Personnel matters, including nonrenewals and dismissals, disciplinary action for unprofessional behavior, involuntary transfers, and turning down staff requests that exceed contract provisions;
- Student appeals of decisions related to discipline and academic standing, including graduation; and
- Budget cuts that negatively affect students and staff.

Each of the superintendents identified personnel as the top area for difficult decision making. One respondent said, "The really tough ones are always personnel and generally involve firing people."

One way or another, each of them identified personnel as the top area for difficult decision making. For example, one respondent said, "The really tough ones are always personnel and generally involve firing people." A second replied, "Firings are the toughest."

Several others cited specific personnel cases, captured by these quotes:

- "I had a difficult time with one of our principals and had to decide to move him, which meant moving someone else. He is a very good soul but just not getting the job done. My decision created a community uproar with screaming and yelling, but I decided it had to be done and wouldn't back down."
- "When once-competent, caring people have moved beyond their role or can't make a transition, you have to help them see it. Sometimes it has to be done publicly. You are trying to do the right thing for a child. It's different when those [involved] violate their responsibilities to kids. Then the decision is easier."
- "I had to clean house by getting rid of ineffective administrators. It was hard because of their families, but I had to do it for the kids."
- "I chose a principal who wasn't the popular choice because I knew it was right."

With regard to student matters, superintendents described such cases as being difficult because, as one participant said, "There's the conflict of having to be the bad guy in instances where faculty and staff interests conflict with those of students." Another said, "With student appeals of suspensions, my heart goes out to the kid, but I have to support the principal."

On the topic of decisions related to budget cutting, one of the superintendents captured the essence of everyone's responses: "When you have to cut the budget, you have to decide what to cut and what to preserve. You have to cut people, often good people." And budget cuts appear to have caused the superintendents to bend more than some of the other issues. As one said, "With the budget sometimes, I rationalize by saying it's their town and schools, but it's tough to make the decision to cut. I may have to stretch without really compromising." Another participant commented, "When it comes to things like budget [cuts], it's a question of doing the least harm. Knowing they are hurtful, I have to make a decision and sort out what will do the least harm."

Asked whether they had ever compromised their basic values when making tough decisions, by and large, the superintendents said no. But some provided further clarification, which indicated that it was less about sacrificing their basic values and more about understanding the reality of the political environment, recognizing the need to make progress incrementally, and acknowledging differing values. As one stated, "Compromise may not be about values but about success, or the greater good, because of politics. You bump up against [different] values of what is educationally sound." Along the same lines, another said, "Sometimes you have to compromise, but it's a matter of degree. But not on the big ones."

One superintendent also acknowledged the importance of the political environment when he stated, "I have never been threatened with the loss of my job. Part of it is establishing who you are and operating with integrity. You can only lose it [integrity] once." Another said, "I don't compromise my values. I may compromise my pride. I'm not always right. I may have to look at it again. I never compromise on safety and security. If something is not contractual, and if the greater good is not affected, then individual compromises are possible."

In the preceding paragraph, a superintendent talked about being in a setting that didn't require him to compromise his values or threaten his job. In the following excerpt, a superintendent talks about the pressures of a more threatening environment:

> I can't think of a time in this job. In another position, I dealt with a board that was extremely difficult. I was in survival mode, trying to get through things when everything I knew to work, didn't. The board tried to embarrass [me], so I had to

orchestrate more carefully. When dealing with a board you can't trust and who are difficult, you end up doing less. You don't stick your neck out; you're less of a leader. Looking back, I grew, I learned, grew stronger, and gained confidence. I accomplished some good things, but I could have done much more.

WHAT GUIDES SUPERINTENDENTS' DECISION MAKING?

In their book, *Why We Believe What We Believe: Uncovering Our Biological Need for Meaning, Spirituality, and Truth,* authors Newberg and Waldman (2006) wrote, "Beliefs govern nearly every aspect of our lives. They tell us how to pray and how to vote, whom to trust and whom to avoid; and they shape our personal behaviors and spiritual ethics throughout life" (p. 5).

All of the superintendents interviewed described a set of beliefs within which they operate.

All of the superintendents interviewed described a set of beliefs within which they operate. One said, "I try to be fair and operate with integrity. Others might not agree, but in my own mind I need to feel I have operated above board. I work hard to earn trust." A second remarked, "What I think is best for kids. It's an easy philosophy, though not in practice because of politics." A third observed, "I weigh 'harm to self versus harm to others.' With self, I look at remediation and intervention, unless there's a threat to the common good. If the safety or security of the whole is at stake, the person has got to go." A fourth replied, "I have to do the right thing insofar as I know it. It helps if I can identify what is good for adults or kids. Kids have to come first." Someone else offered, "Saul Cooperman said something like, 'Never for the sake of peace and quiet deny your convictions and experience.' I try to live this way." Another put it simply, "I rely on my values and the spiritual piece. When it's crazy outside, I have to look inside for strength and inner peace." Yet another summed it up by saying, "When we were vacationing in Hawaii, I saw the Hawaiian definition of perfection, called *kina' ole,* which is 'doing the right thing, in the right way, at the right time, in the right place, to the right person, for the right reason, with the right feeling . . . the first time.' I think about that a lot."

So what guides superintendents in making tough decisions and acting on them? Deciding what's best for kids, with fairness and integrity, while being trustworthy; balancing individual interests and the common good, while ensuring safety and security; and following a variation of the Hippocratic oath to be helpful and not harmful.

WHERE DO SUPERINTENDENTS' BASIC VALUES COME FROM?

All of the superintendents pointed to family and religious upbringing as the two primary components in the development of their basic values, with a heavy emphasis on service to others. One superintendent captured it briefly and humorously when she said, "My parents and the Church. I have guilt that won't quit, between Catholic guilt and Italian guilt." Another superintendent credited his family with instilling in him the belief that "education is the gateway to opportunity and [the means] for making a difference," as well as "the notion of service." He went on to talk about his parochial school education, especially high school, where the Jesuits taught him he'd have to be one of "the men and women [in service] for others," and that "there are things we ought to do." Someone else said, "The way I was brought up—my formative years had a cumulative effect. Neither of my parents went beyond eighth grade. They were older, and their age and maturity contributed to my values." He also talked about his education when he shared,

All of the superintendents pointed to family and religious upbringing as the two primary components in the development of their basic values, with a heavy emphasis on service to others.

"I had a parochial education and attended a service academy for one year. Both were an indoctrination, and my basic values come from a religious base."

The other superintendents provided comparable stories. One female superintendent offered the following:

Home. . . . I saw models like my father, who was dedicated to his work. My family had core values [such as] fairness and treating people with respect. Schooling. . . . In Catholic schools, I learned to take the high road, honesty, servitude. [She made a side comment about starting to take care of herself, as if this were somehow antithetical to service to others.]

Another respondent said,

My family. . . . They weren't wealthy, but they helped the family down the street at Christmas and their niece, with nursing school. They contributed to the community through serving on town boards. My father helped build ramps for the disabled. The Church was a part of our lives, and we followed the rules as Catholics. We were good Catholics, but not really religious. It was an influence, part of how my values were formed, but I'm more liberal than the Catholic Church. The rituals are still comforting, and I enjoy being a part of it.

This is how this superintendent reported developing her values:

From my strong family background, I learned about helping other people, honesty, being someone people can trust, sticking together, and working together to do what needs to be done. I had a Catholic school education—strong values and guilt. I know what's right and wrong, which was ingrained.

A couple of superintendents pointed to other influences, though less dominant than their families and religious backgrounds, which affected their values development. One talked about "people within education whom I'd regard as great thinkers and heroes, who have stood up and made a difference for kids." And another said, "Since adolescence, I have done a lot of reading and find nobility in certain characters."

As a former English teacher, I have to admit this resonated with me. Editors Singer and Singer captured it well in the introduction to their anthology, *The Moral of the Story: An Anthology of Ethics Through Literature* (2005), when they wrote,

Long before the rise of systematic philosophical thought, however, people have been making up stories in order to convey what they think about how we ought to live. Inevitably, in telling stories, and in writing novels, plays, short stories, and poems, the authors and narrators raise moral questions and suggest possible ways of answering them. (p. x)

I find that there's a parallel between the aforementioned stories in literature and poetry and my collection of superintendents' stories because the latter provides an insider's view of the issues confronting superintendents and some possible ways of addressing them. I believe that current superintendents can learn something from these stories, perhaps finding some resonance with their own values and ways of thinking, or maybe even finding some comfort in seeing others grappling with some of the same tough decisions. I should think new or aspiring superintendents would find the stories interesting and potentially useful, too.

Do Superintendents See a Difference Between Being "Religious" and Being "Spiritual"?

In *The Spiritual Dimension of Leadership: 8 Key Principles to Leading More Effectively,* Paul Houston and Steve Sokolow (2006) differentiate between religion and spirituality as outlined below:

> There's some confusion about spirituality. Many people see spirituality and religion as being the same thing. We suggest a different lens, one that uses a metaphor of the pipes. You can have different kinds of pipes: copper pipes, plastic pipes, lead pipes, round pipes, oval pipes, big pipes and small. As we see it, the pipes represent religion in all its various forms, with different specifications to those forms based on theology, history, and practice. Only one substance, however, flows through those pipes, and what flows through is the essence of spirituality. Different religions may call that essence different things. But whether you call it divine intelligence, universal awareness, divine wisdom, conscience, or our moral guidance system, it's still spirituality. The difference between religion and spirituality is the difference between form and substance. What we are talking about is the essence of the personal relationship between you and the Divine, whether you're a Buddhist or a Baptist or a person of any other faith, or no organized faith at all. (p. xxiii)

Regarding the difference between religion and spirituality, many of the superintendents drew a similar conclusion to that of Houston and Sokolow, though a couple of them expressed the belief that one still can be spiritual without necessarily believing in a Higher Power. One person said that "religion is spirituality with a heavy set of dogma, a moral center beyond self," while spirituality is "living according to a moral compass or guide that has developed within me, but minus the dogma." She went on to say that "a belief in a Higher Power is important."

A different superintendent remarked that "being religious is tied to a particular doctrine, a view of man's relationship with God defined by certain life stations that are kind of pathways: Baptism, Confirmation, Bar Mitzvah, and so on." He said that "being spiritual involves a series of concentric circles from self and one's relationship to God, to family, to community, to the larger community." Another respondent said, "Being religious is orthodoxy, a set of dogma; it's man-made. Spiritual is believing in God or Other Spirit, a Higher Being." Yet another defined the difference as follows: "Being religious has to do with the Church, what the Catholic Church tells me I should be, the rituals and the rules. Spiritual is a belief in God, some kind of afterlife or reward, something after death."

A couple of the superintendents expressed the belief that being spiritual is seeing oneself as part of something bigger, something beyond oneself.

A couple of the superintendents expressed the belief that being spiritual is seeing oneself as part of something bigger, something beyond oneself. For example, one participant said that "being religious is believing in God in a formalized manner," while "spirituality is the belief there's a greater meaning to things, that there's a purpose to life beyond self." Yet another spoke of a religious person as being "someone who has fairly specific beliefs about God, which are associated with organized religion—Catholic, Protestant, Muslim," while being spiritual is "being part of something that's larger than yourself but not tied into a religion that's inflexible."

A few of the superintendents consider themselves religious as well as spiritual. For example, one participant said, "Religion is somewhat important, though the rules and regulations aren't. A belief in a Higher Power is [important]. Spirituality is very important in my life. Being spiritual is being ethical and moral, making decisions based on that." A second commented, "I am a practicing Catholic living with a notion of social justice and service. There are certain aspects [of religion] that are very important and others, not at all. The Liturgical part, the sacraments and symbols, are still very important because they are life station events." He went on to talk about reconciling his ties to the church with his aversion to the behavior of priests.

He wasn't the only one of the superintendents struggling with this issue. Another made the following remarks on the same topic: "As I grew older, the model of priests mediating morality became problematic. I still feel the need for a spiritual dimension in my life. I like being a searcher rather than [following] something I'm told to believe." A fourth superintendent also expressed dissatisfaction with the disparity between religious teachings and the behavior of followers, though not specific to priests. A fifth participant indicated he had pulled away from the Church without identifying a specific reason and talking about the empty space that has resulted when he said, "I'm not religious, but I am spiritual. Maybe it's rebellion. I feel a void. . . . Religion is not central to my life. Spirituality is, to the extent I try to live a good life with dignity."

A different superintendent phrased her feelings about religion and spirituality this way:

> I don't think I feel a great yearning to belong to something greater [religion]. I can't imagine myself going back to childhood beliefs. I'm more interested in intellectual pursuit with people who are good people. Spirituality is a lot harder to define, and I haven't thought a lot about it. I would like to find a place where people talk about issues that are important to ethical choices and moral decisions and being part of something that's larger than myself but not tied into a religion that's inflexible. I'm not sure if there is a God anymore, but there's a realm larger than little me. I'm part of something else and should spend a lifetime trying to be a better person all the time.

One respondent expressed very strong feelings about her early negative experiences with her church, which caused her to separate from any religious affiliation. She said, "I hate organized religion, and it's not a part of my life. I don't have a feeling about a Greater Being, but I'm intrigued with Unitarianism and listen to the service on the radio. It's so different from what I grew up on. And [I read] books on Buddhism."

I found it interesting that a number of the superintendents saw their roles as ministerial in nature. One described education as "missionary" work. Another superintendent provided this view of his role:

> Some of what we do has a pastoral quality to it in the best sense of the concept. We are called upon to bring the community

together in a public way. There is an expectation that we will be responsible for symbolic leadership in a positive way without being orthodox. It happens in different ways such as [at] retirements, memorial services, and graduations.

When I listed the superintendents whom I intended to invite to take part in my conversations about spirituality, I had no idea that all but two of them had been raised Catholic, with one of the remaining two educated in Catholic schools and clearly influenced by those teachings in terms of the formation of her values.

Do Religion and/or Spirituality Play a Role in Superintendents' Decision Making?

Clearly, all of the superintendents saw that their decision making was and is tied to their religious upbringing and/or their spirituality, as they defined it. Because those definitions varied, their responses did as well. Some of them also noted that they are not cognizant of their religious or spiritual beliefs in their decision making because it happens automatically. As one participant observed, "I don't think about it; it's who I am. I may reflect on it [later], but I don't think about it while making decisions." A second phrased it this way: "I'm not conscious about it in terms of religion and spirituality on a day-to-day basis, but as guiding principles that become part of who you are and [that] no longer have to be spoken." A third summed it up when she said, "Probably enormously in the end because it [religion and spirituality] fashions who you are."

To the same question, one of the other participants remarked,

It's in me every day. If I see an injustice, I get outraged and speak out rather than let it go. It comes from deep in my soul, and is what makes me human and connected to the rest of the world. I believe in God and "Golden Rule" values. It gets you through the difficult times. . . . The spiritual piece is visceral for me. I feel it when I'm helping those in need, or I'm really successful at work.

Another made the following comments:

I think leadership requires reflection. . . . You need to know who you are, what your motives are. Sometimes you're doing it [decision making] on the fly and have to slow down to gain perspective. In this job I have lots of doubt, while having to appear confident and solid because the community expects it of you. There's always doubt, but you can't allow it to paralyze you. . . . You can't become overly confident or ego-driven. Spirituality allows you to reflect.

Finally, one superintendent offered the following thoughts:

I struggle with how to pass on the spiritual side of what we do. How do we share with the next generation who will replace us? How will they find resiliency for dealing with personal crises? Some would seek therapy, but I tend to be more "mystical." I need to go inside to sort things out—more spiritual, contemplative— and then bring it back to discuss.

In the end, all of the superintendents said that they try to do the right thing, particularly as it relates to the best interests of students, and based on their basic values—values grounded in family and religious upbringing.

Summary

As a school superintendent, I struggle with the difficult decisions that are part and parcel of my job. I have sometimes wondered if I am the only one who experiences this struggle and the self-doubt that comes with it. I also have wondered if one day I'll be "found out" as being less informed and less sure than I often appear to be. When I do make decisions, they are based on my notion of what's right, which is born of my own basic values. Like the other superintendents, my basic values grew out of my family and religious background. Although now I am not a religious person per se, I do believe I am a spiritual one. And that factors into my decision making and my actions as a superintendent.

Earlier in this chapter, I talked about earlier research of mine, which concluded that superintendents take their organizations forward based on "who you are," and wondered whether superintendents' decisions also are tied to "who you are." If they are, they would have to be tied to their values, which come from family and religious roots. To confirm this, I wanted to find out what drives the decision making and administrative actions of other practicing superintendents and whether or not religion and spirituality are factors. So I employed a process of interviews, which allowed me to understand the superintendents' experiences by gathering their stories. Based on the stories of the nine I interviewed, I believe the answer to my question about whether or not their decision making is based on "who you are" is an unequivocal yes and that "who you are" comes down to character, which is developed in relationship to family and religious upbringing. As a result, leadership in the superintendency is values-based, and therefore, past experience determines current behavior relative to decision making and action in the role of superintendent.

One superintendent said it well when she commented, "We don't take enough time to talk about this with one another."

Although it was unintentional and unanticipated, all but one of the superintendents had some affiliation with the Catholic Church. However, the one superintendent who did not have such an affiliation (but did have a religious upbringing) shared the same characteristics as the others, which indicates that religious upbringing, of whatever sort, affects the character development of the individual. I believe that superintendents raised in any religious tradition would share similar values and views as the ones whom I interviewed.

A number of themes arose from the stories. The notions of "what's best for the kids" and "doing what's right" were voiced emphatically and repeatedly by the respondents. These are clearly the driving forces behind their decision making and administrative actions. At the same time, they said that, though they may gather information and listen to others in determining a course of action, they ultimately determine for themselves what's right based on their own basic values. Even in the face of political pressure or public outcry, they reported that they won't back down. They acknowledged having to compromise because of the political nature of their jobs, but not when it came to their fundamental values.

The participants all voiced self-doubt and acknowledged that they aren't always right. They also said they have to make decisions and take action even in the face of that doubt, with the possibility of being wrong and the resulting consequences, which they do not take lightly.

They talked about the need for affirmation, which rarely comes, and so they often must look inward to find solace in past successes. They want to leave a legacy, both in terms of the children they serve and the next generation of educational leaders who will replace them.

When all is said and done, these superintendents operate from a set of firmly held beliefs, which they acknowledge stemmed primarily from their parents and religious training. Some of them see themselves as both religious and spiritual, while others have left behind organized religion. All of them, without exception, consider themselves to be spiritual according to their own definition of what that means. All of them see the influence of religion and spirituality in their role as superintendent. In addition, they all talked about the importance of reflection in judging the soundness of their decisions and actions.

Although all had reservations about the likelihood that they would have anything of value to offer on the topic of spirituality in educational leadership, each expressed satisfaction at the conclusion of our conversation. One superintendent said it well when she commented, "We don't take enough time to talk about this with one another."

I think she's right.

References

Barth, R. S. (2003). *Lessons learned: Shaping relationships and the culture of the workplace*. Thousand Oaks, CA: Corwin Press.

Houston, P. D., & Sokolow, S. L. (2006). *The spiritual dimension of leadership: 8 keys to leading more effectively.* Thousand Oaks, CA: Corwin Press.

Newberg, A., & Waldman, M. R. (2006). *Why we believe what we believe: Uncovering our biological need for meaning, spirituality, and truth.* New York: Free Press.

Seidman, I. E. (1991). *Interviewing as qualitative research: A guide for researchers in education and the social sciences.* New York: Teachers College Press.

Sheff Kohn, C. L. (1995). *Exploratory case study of the power problem of the superintendency.* Ann Arbor: University of Michigan.

Singer, P., & Singer, R. (Eds.). (2005). *The moral of the story: An anthology of ethics through literature.* Malden, MA: Blackwell.

CHAPTER SEVEN

PERSONAL GROWTH IN THE WORKPLACE

Spiritual Practices You Can Use

CHRISTA METZGER

The inspiration for this chapter came from a little lizard. I was sitting on my designated meditation bench near our home in the forest by the Neuse River in North Carolina. With notepad on my lap and pen in my hand, I closed my eyes for a few moments, waiting for inspiration. When I opened them, there he was: a little brownish lizard, who I suspected had taken over "my" meditation bench while I had been working and teaching in Los Angeles for the past 3 months. I could see his head and half of his body over the top of my notepad. His eyes (Have you ever noticed how a lizard's eyes can turn in any direction while the head stays still?) were looking straight at me. We stared at each other for a long time. I didn't move. Apparently deciding that I posed no threat, he slowly crawled up onto my notepad, and then changed his color to green. I'm not sure what that means in lizard body language, but in my childhood I was taught that the color green signifies hope. So I give credit to my little lizard as my companion spirit in this work.

PERSONAL GROWTH AND SPIRITUAL LEADERSHIP

This chapter is an extension of the book I recently completed, *Balancing Leadership and Personal Growth* (Metzger, 2006). Although I learned a lot from my research for this book about what leaders do to balance their lives, I was left with an unanswered question: How do leaders engage in their own personal growth and develop their spirituality—not only on their own time, but also in the place where they work, on the job, during their workday? So I began to ask school administrators and other educational leaders if this was possible and how it might be done. The results of that investigation are the basis of this chapter.

I use the term "Personal Growth" as a tangible way to explore how the spiritual dimensions of leadership might be developed and nurtured. Personal Growth has to do with how leaders cultivate the inner and personal dimensions of their being so as to gain a more balanced and meaningful life (Metzger, 2006). Being in balance is essential if one is to respond effectively to the stresses and crises that are a part of *every* life, and the stress-filled life of a school administrator is certainly no exception. My premise is that when individual leaders pay attention to all dimensions of their being, they will be able to fulfill their purpose as leaders as well as find meaning in all aspects of their lives.

Being in balance is essential if one is to respond effectively to the stresses and crises that are a part of every life, and the stress-filled life of a school administrator is certainly no exception.

In the past, during my many years as a principal and a superintendent, we avoided using such terms as "spirituality" or "soul." In recent years, however, I have seen this change because of the courage of some who have begun to write and talk about the importance of this vital dimension of leadership. The reader may want to consult other works that provide a thoughtful and detailed discussion of the terminology surrounding the word "spiritual" (Covey, 2004; Houston & Sokolow, 2006, p. xxiii; Metzger, 2006, p. 17). You may also be interested in what Thomas Moore, the well-known author of *Care of the Soul* (1992), wrote in a recent issue of *Spirituality and Health* on "The Spirituality in Leadership" (Moore, 2006).

Personal Growth is a process that involves the inner life, the heart and soul of the leader; it is his or her personal identity, the ground from which actions and decisions arise. In that sense, it is a "spiritual" search to connect the human spirit with the wellspring of one's deepest being—the Universal Spirit, Higher Power, God, the Tao, Creator, Allah, or whatever one may choose to call this ultimate source, the central mystery and the origin of all things. This inner spiritual search is manifested in outer behavior and actions. There are both internal processes and external activities involved in engaging in one's Personal Growth.

SIX THEMES THAT DEFINE PERSONAL GROWTH

Personal Growth has to do with what you do for yourself, for your inner development. The school superintendents, college deans, principals, and other administrators who participated in my national study (Metzger, 2006) used the following terms to define Personal Growth:

Balance: Balancing life and work, professional and personal life, prioritizing and using time wisely

Self-Actualization: Self-confidence, being happy, taking care of oneself, having an authentic existence, becoming a fully functioning person, having an internal measure of success

Personal Improvement: Growing, renewal, learning, and developing oneself from within

Values: Clarity of personal beliefs, character, integrity, knowing and prioritizing one's values, knowing oneself and one's limits, being in tune with oneself

Inner Focus: Sense of inner peace, of heart, of being grounded and centered; spiritual peace; having meaning in life; looking at the whole person, especially the inner person; living with soul

Relationships: Leadership inspired by personal vision; being reflective about one's relationship to work, attending to one's own needs as well as serving others, knowing how to take criticism, identifying what can be controlled and living within that

STRATEGIES FOR PERSONAL GROWTH

In addition to insights on defining what is meant by Personal Growth, six strategies emerged from my study (Metzger, 2006). The practices and activities that administrators used to engage in their Personal Growth included the following six areas, listed in the approximate order of how frequently they were used by various kinds of educational leaders:

- Spending time with family and friends
- Physical activities—exercise, diversions
- Reading—reflective, recreational, spiritual
- Time spent in silence, solitude, and meditation
- Creative work—art, music, writing, and hobbies
- Dreams—pursuing dreams and learning from night dreams

When I asked administrators about the times they set aside to practice such activities for their Personal Growth, most of them reported that they used these strategies outside of their workday. For example, administrators took time in the mornings, evenings, or on weekends for themselves, and for their Personal Growth.

How, then, might leaders engage in Personal Growth practices during their workday, thus enhancing both their personal and professional lives?

If one accepts the assumption that Personal Growth strategies provide paths to build the "inner" (spiritual) capacities of the leader, it would be important for leaders to find ways of incorporating such strategies throughout their day— and maybe especially in the workplace. How, then, might leaders engage in Personal Growth practices during their workday, thus enhancing both their personal and professional lives? Specifically, I wanted to further explore the following questions:

- To what extent is it possible to incorporate Personal Growth practices into the working lives of school leaders?
- What Personal Growth practices, if any, are administrators using during their workday?
- How do leaders develop and express their spirituality on the job, in the workplace?
- How might such practices be manifested in the leader's daily life on the job?

Personal Growth Strategies— 2007 Research Results

Using a one-page survey and some interviews, I asked two questions of administrators from all levels of schooling, including K–12 administrators and higher education faculty and administrators. I also surveyed a small group of business executives. I have included their responses with those of educational leaders and have referenced a few of them separately if they seemed atypical from those who work in an educational environment. The two questions were these:

1. How do you take care of yourself?

2. What do you do *during your workday* for your own personal growth?

The survey began with the following introduction:

Being a leader is often a stressful job. Many administrators are too busy to pay attention to their own physical, emotional, mental, and spiritual side. Research has shown that when administrators engage in activities for their own personal growth, it is usually done outside of the workday. Such activities might include creative work (art, music, writing), physical exercise, reflective reading, hobbies, finding times alone (e.g., meditation), and spending time with friends and family.

I then asked the respondents to

Please list anything that helps you to be in balance, nurture yourself, renew yourself, relax in times of stress, be centered and focused, know who you are, and become a more fully functioning person.

A total of 89 responses were returned by various groups as shown in Table 7.1 on page 116.

Table 7.1   Survey Respondents

Leadership position	Number of respondents
Principals and assistant principals	26
Higher education administrators	23
Higher education faculty	17
Business leaders	10
District-level administrators	9
Others (site coaches, teachers)	4

One interesting finding was that, though this information was not specifically requested on the survey form, many respondents also wanted to tell me what practices they used *on their own time.* Thus, many of them expanded their answers to cover both the personal and professional aspects of their lives. Let me address those responses first.

When I compared the activities the respondents listed for their Personal Growth done *outside* of the workday, I found them to be very similar to the six strategies that arose from my 2006 study (as referenced above). Below is a list of the practices respondents reported using outside of their workday. These are shown in order of frequency, beginning with the ones mentioned most often. The number following the item indicates how many times it was cited by various respondents.

Nonworkday Personal Growth Practices

- Reading (spiritual, reflective, recreational): 14
- Time with family and friends, talk with spouse: 12
- Regular exercise, working out (e.g., yoga, aerobics, walking): 11
- Hobbies, diversions (making jewelry, woodworking, scrapbooking, shopping, handicrafts, guitar, piano): 6
- Relaxing at end of day (e.g., watching comedy shows, TV programs, or movies; glass of wine at end of day): 5
- Spending time/laughing with my children or grandchildren: 4
- Time to pamper myself (facial, hot tub, hot showers, manicure/pedicure): 4
- Taking drives (car, motorcycle) in nature: 4

- Relaxing with my animals, walking the dogs: 4
- Church activities: 3
- Nice (candlelight) dinners with spouse: 2
- Good night's sleep: 2
- Cooking: 2
- Time alone to relax or meditate: 2
- Writing (journal): 2
- Volunteer work: 1
- Playing games on my computer: 1
- Having a few drinks with friends: 1
- Going to movies and theater: 1
- Travel: 1

Personal Growth Practices Used During the Workday

The results of my 2007 study show clearly that leaders are incorporating Personal Growth practices into their workday. Only one respondent stated that this was difficult to do, and one person simply replied, "This is a very good question." Although my research is based on a limited sample, the findings provide hope that leaders are coming to be aware of the importance of paying attention to themselves, of developing their own inner and spiritual dimensions—and that they're finding it's possible to do this as part of everyday life, even at work.

An important element in the activities mentioned by the respondents was the connection between inner processes and external actions. Most of the reported activities included a combination of physical, spiritual, mental, and emotional dimensions and some type of external setting. For example, centering and reflecting before a stressful meeting or an impending decision is an *internal*

My findings provide hope that leaders are coming to be aware of the importance of developing their own inner and spiritual dimensions—and that they're finding it's possible to do this as part of everyday life, even at work.

activity; however, suggestions as to how this might be accomplished involve *external* surroundings or actions by the individual. For example, to reflect and focus on a situation might involve any of the following specific actions: closing the office door for a few moments, taking a walk outside, discussing it with a trusted friend, reading something reflectively, looking at a photograph, breathing, praying, closing one's eyes, or listening to soothing music.

PERSONAL GROWTH PRACTICES— THE INTERNAL PROCESS

What does an "internal process" include? It essentially means engaging with the spiritual, mental, and emotional aspects of your being. In the following paragraphs, I provide an example that illustrates how this internal process might work. It may be used as an exercise for any situation or decision on which you wish to reflect—especially one about which you may feel some conflict, or a dilemma that leaves you unclear about an appropriate course of action. At first, you will want to take adequate time to move deliberately and slowly through the list of questions below. After you grow accustomed to making decisions by working through such an internal process, it will take you less time and may even become almost automatic.

First, select a situation or a decision on which you wish to reflect. Choose a quiet time and a space where you can be still with your thoughts and feelings. You may wish to close your office door or sit in a quiet place. Begin by noticing something in your surroundings that helps you to become centered and to take a different perspective. Use one or more of your senses to assist you in this process: look at a picture, smell a favorite fragrance, listen to music, touch a plant or an object in your office, or just sit (or walk, if that works better for you) and observe yourself breathing in and out. Allow yourself to experience quietly the situation that is troubling you.

Notice the feelings and thoughts that arise about the situation. This internal process involves both your head and your heart. Ask yourself the following questions:

- What is the right thing to do in this situation?
- What does my intuition (gut feeling) tell me?
- What does my intellect (reason, logic) tell me?
- What are all the factors (considerations) to which I need to pay attention? (These might include your own standards, laws, and procedures, as well as others' needs.)
- Which of these factors are the most important in this situation?
- What will maintain and build my own integrity and enhance my mission as a leader?

- What are my highest values to which I want to be true, and how will they affect the situation?
- What are the goals of my organization that I need to consider?
- What will best meet others' needs while still adhering to accepted procedures, legal requirements, and my own principles?

After you have reflected on these questions (or even while you're doing it), write down some notes of what occurs to you. Don't try too hard to organize your thoughts and impressions. Just ask yourself this: What does my situation feel like now, and what kind of actions might I take? You may receive only partial insights the first time and feel the need to repeat the process. Allow these questions to be with you, and give yourself time to continue focusing on them until your course of action becomes clear to you.

PERSONAL GROWTH PRACTICES— THE EXTERNAL ACTIONS

The "external process" involves something that you *do*—an outward action that will enhance the success of the work you do internally. Here is a summary of the external factors mentioned most frequently by leaders who used them while practicing Personal Growth in their workplace:

- *The environment:* Is your office atmosphere conducive to Personal Growth and spiritual practices? For example, are there inspirational sayings posted, photos of family, plants or flowers? Is there a minimum of clutter, and is the furniture arranged to permit desirable interaction with others? Can you listen to your favorite music for relaxation or stimulation, if that helps you? Can you take walks outside and gain a new perspective from nature or from those who may cross your path?

- *Finding personal time and space:* Is there a private, personal space for you to sit or walk when you need quiet, uninterrupted moments to reflect—either in your office or outside? Do you schedule your time in accordance with what's most important for you? Do you take breaks or time for lunch? If so, how are you using those breaks? Do you close your door sometimes—even for just a few moments? Do you find time to read, to exercise, to meditate on or to contemplate something?

- *Connecting with colleagues and friends:* Are there opportunities to share time with the important others in your life? Do you have meals with others? Do you take time to connect by e-mail or telephone with friends, colleagues, or family members during the workday? Do you walk around your campus or workplace to touch the lives of others, including colleagues, staff, and students? Do you share with, listen to, or simply spend time with people who inspire you? Do you have someone you trust with whom you can discuss your concerns? (Note how connecting with others also has an "internal" element in terms of what you do or say with them.)

CONNECTING THE INNER AND OUTER— INTERNAL AND EXTERNAL FACTORS

The following section shows the specific practices listed by administrators in the exact words and phrases they used. Even though there is some repetition, I believe that using the respondents' own words will prove to be a more powerful way to evoke your own unique and creative ideas for putting these suggestions to work in your life. I have organized them into major themes—both in terms of the type of activity and in order of how often they were mentioned.

The most important strategy in connecting the Inner and Outer is to do something to create the setting (external activity) for your inner spiritual development (internal processes) to take place.

As you read the responses, note how they connect "internal" activities to an "external" setting. Each requires some type of external engagement— an activity within which the internal process can take place. Many of the internal processes may be engaged in through various outer actions. For example, while taking a walk you may connect with others or you may meditate. Closing your office door allows you to engage in a physical activity, listen to music, read, or connect with others via e-mail or phone. Lunchtime is a good time to do all of these. Reading requires setting aside some time for this essentially internal activity. Taking a break will be useful for any of the other activities, but you must be willing and able to make time for one.

The most important strategy in connecting the Inner and Outer is to do something to create the setting (external activity) for your inner spiritual development (internal processes) to take place.

As I mentioned above, a profound finding of this study was that there are so many choices and options for engaging in Personal Growth practices during the workday. The lists below are not copied from some book; they show what leaders are actually doing in their daily lives. A common element in all of the practices is that *everyday activities may be used for the purpose of contacting the "other"—the spiritual part of you within.* This is the essence of Personal Growth. You will gain new perspectives by focusing on your inner self—if only for a few moments during your workday. You have the power to get in touch with something other than your immediate situation. You may find renewal by connecting with others, or by being alone. You can grow as a person and a leader in all dimensions of your being. There are plenty of activities to adapt that will suit your personal leadership style and your particular work environment.

PERSONAL GROWTH PRACTICES DURING THE WORKDAY— SUGGESTIONS FROM PRACTITIONERS

In listing the practices below, I have included every comment made on the surveys and in the interviews by the respondents. My goal was to learn what practices administrators are using, not to judge the extent to which any of these might contribute to their Personal Growth or enhance their effectiveness as leaders. That is the subject for another study. I felt that it was important to learn first what leaders did, in response to the questions asked about their own Personal Growth during the workday. As this list shows, there are many ways in which this is being accomplished. The numbers in parentheses indicate how many times that idea was mentioned by respondents.

Connect With Others (45)

Find another professional to talk to	Connect with colleagues (personally, e-mail, lunch, phone)
Take a walk to talk in person with someone in another department instead of calling or e-mailing	Personal e-mail or phone call (reach out)
Ask others for advice and suggestions	Brainstorm educational issues
Talk to coworkers	Debrief stressful situations with a colleague
Call a nurturing person on the phone	Write a brief note to someone important in my life
Connect with each person at my work (share time), take time to get to know people	Connect with positive, inspiring people every week
Plan connections with friends and loved ones	Listen to staff (and students)
Stay connected with students, walk through classrooms and talk to kids	Smile at everyone I meet—to spread cheer
Call or e-mail a friend or my spouse	Text message with my kids, my wife; call during the day
Regular standing "one o'clock meeting" with assistant principal (chat informally)	Reflective conversations with thoughtful people
Joke with colleagues	Mentor classes/students [from a business executive]
End of day—actively involved with student sports teams	Advise and guide teachers

Walk (29)

Walk around campus, enjoy nature, smell the air, observe people	Talk with kids on playgrounds
Walk into classrooms	Look at leaves and flowers—bring one back to office
Use walking time for quiet meditation	Walk on my street—marvel at the beauty of the trees

Music (21)

Play and listen to music in the office: soft, good, favorite, my kind of music

Reflection and Self-Talk (18)

Stay positive	Remind myself of my goals
Think of new ways to reach my goals and dreams	Before a stressful meeting, look at pictures of my family
Do deep breathing exercises, especially in times of stress	Check in on my intuitive and gut instincts
Keep a sense of humor	Take some quiet time to focus
Remind myself that this job is not all there is to my life and future	Reframe situations (look at crisis from other person's point of view)
Reflect on strategies/procedures concerning stressful situations	Help others achieve their goals and dreams
Remember that no decision needs to be made immediately	Laugh and soak in the small amounts of praise that may come my way [from a site-level administrator]

Lunch Time (16)

Have lunch with teachers (to stay on top of their issues)	Lunch in office
Lunch out of office (walk to snack shop)	Do non–work-related activities at lunch
2–3 days a week spend time away, e.g., window shopping (I have more stamina in the afternoon when I do that.)	Take time to eat lunch—at least 15 minutes with no interruptions
Visit staff—school or personal conversations	Walk during lunch, walk my dogs
Lunch and recess times—be out with students	Try to leave the office for lunch to meet a friend, a colleague, or my spouse

Close Your Door (16)

Eat a snack or lunch and read something	Nap
Make a cup of tea and enjoy it at my desk	Browse Internet for information
Just sit with my thoughts, reflect on the next activity in my day	Look out my window frequently to enjoy the sunshine and trees
Do relaxation exercises (e.g., stretching in my chair)	Breathe deeply when I need "time out" and reflect
Turn off phone/computer, lights, fax	

Read (15)

Always have a book, article, journal to read—even for 5 minutes during breaks	Browse Web sites on philosophical or conceptual issues of interest
Make time for my own scholarship (professional reading), research	Read something not job related (e.g., a self-help book, daily devotional)
Read something to learn new thoughts and different philosophies	Read an inspirational devotional first thing in morning

Take Breaks (14)

Check out news Web sites, inspirational Web sites	Visit classes/playground to interact
Read to students	Visit school sites [from a superintendent]
Play basketball with the kids	Connect with someone and chat
Take a break (leave my desk and computer) and come back with a fresh approach and receptivity to my next conversation	Take small breaks throughout day to relax and to nurture myself

Your Space (11)

Keep my work area as a "meditation" environment (e.g., plants, flowers, fountain, artwork)	Display pictures of meaningful important people (my loved ones)
Look at meaningful things in my office throughout the day	Keep a frog on my desk to remind me of . . .
Spray an apple spice spray in the office—helps me to relax and focus	Post inspirational sayings and signs
Keep office clear of clutter	

Physical Activities (9)

Work out at the gym at lunch; get a massage	Company sponsors wellness program that includes speakers, runs, etc. [from a business executive]
Keep yoga mat in office	Find a quiet place for yoga stretches
Our firm provides yoga classes twice a week at lunchtime [from a business executive]	Put in place a 20-minute aerobics program for entire school community

Time Management (9)

Have some "white calendar" time each day (nothing scheduled)	Come in after hours/Saturday to concentrate on a special project
Stay after everyone has gone to find quiet time	Make a "to do" list and write things down (then let them go)
Make time for what's important to me	Set priorities for myself
Take time to breathe—deeply and slowly	

Meditation (8)

"Transformation comes in the space between breaths, meditation (stationary or physically active)—facilitate access to this space" [from a CEO and founder of a high-tech start-up company]	Do breathing exercises; take a breath to regain an objective perspective
Do visualization and awareness exercises	Chant to focus within and reflect

Prayer (7)

. . . and prayerful moments

Time Alone (7)

Create thought-provoking communications to express myself and share from my heart	View inspirational e-mails and Web sites
Stand outside my office building for five minutes to breathe in fresh air	Sit and rock in my rocking chair
Try to find time alone	Put on TV when staying late

Eating (6)

Eat dark chocolate	Eat snacks
Eat nutritious food	Drink plenty of water

Conferences/Workshops (5)

Attend workshops (sometimes overnight), professional or service organization meetings	Helps to leave immediate job issues behind

CENTERING YOURSELF

In order to live a balanced life, leaders must pay attention to their own Personal Growth, in both their personal and their professional lives. This includes taking time to develop all dimensions of being: physical, emotional, mental, and spiritual.

This chapter has examined how this personal development is being carried out by business executives and by educational leaders (principals, assistant principals, district-level administrators, higher education administrators, university faculty, and teachers and other educational practitioners) during their workday, as well as in their everyday life outside of work. Specific practices, involving both internal processes and external activities, have been included that are being used by a variety of leaders during their workday.

At the heart of all of these processes and activities is the same thing: becoming still and allowing yourself to connect with your spirit. Here is the wellspring of your Personal Growth. In concluding this chapter, I describe a centering process that you may use with any activity you select. It is a step-by-step process for going inside yourself and then back out again to proceed with your external situation, and it involves both internal and external dimensions.

You may use this process in the privacy of your office, or when you sit or take a walk in order to reflect on a decision, situation, or crisis. This process has the power to maximize the impact of any of the Personal Growth activities you may select. You can use this process even when you're in the company of others, though the time you will take to move through these steps will probably be abbreviated. The

> *At the heart of all of these processes and activities is the same thing: becoming still and allowing yourself to connect with your spirit. Here is the wellspring of your Personal Growth.*

first few occasions that you try it, give yourself plenty of time to work through it. You may want to read it aloud to yourself first and reflect on each phrase.

First, try to ensure that you have a few undisturbed minutes alone in a private space. Then think of a situation that is stressful for you, a decision about which you feel ambiguous, or a crisis you're facing. Once this process becomes automatic for you, you can use it—in a short or longer version—in almost any situation that requires you to concentrate with your whole being in order to arrive at your best action. Using a memory device always helps me to remember a series. You may want to remember this process by its key words:

1. Clear

2. Center

3. Awareness

4. Present Moment

5. Action

6. Compassion

1. *Clear* your head of mental noise. Let go of thoughts, espe-cially those about your immediate issue; let them pass through you without focusing on them. Engage your other senses, and make space for a new perspective. *Look* at something such as a painting, a photo, or an object, and become engrossed in it by focusing on it and even *touching* it; *visualize* a scene and actually be present there in your imagination; *listen* to some music and notice how it affects you, how it makes you feel; mindfully eat or drink something; engage in a *hands-on* creative project and become completely involved in that. Use a meditation practice to help you *be present* in the moment. Even focusing on your breathing in and out will create some needed distance from your external situation. (You might even discover your own little lizard to give you inspiration.)

2. *Center* yourself and get in touch with your inner resources. You may wish to close your eyes at this point. Find that inner wis-dom, your intuition; pray for guidance; be grateful for the answers you will receive; use your heart (feelings, intuition) to reflect on whatever it is in your path that you need to address. Don't judge or analyze—just allow the situation to be with you. A visualization may help you to get in touch with your intuitive sense and to connect with the spiritual powers within you.

3. *Awareness:* Be fully aware of who you are—your values, pri-orities, and moral principles. Seek inner clarity on what is important to you, what concerns you, what you are afraid of, who your "inner" guides are, and how your divine presence is with you in this moment; sense what is necessary for you to be in balance in this sit-uation. Connect with your spiritual Higher Power and allow it to become a part of who you want to be.

4. *Present Moment:* Return to the "now," the situation at hand. Be aware of how the external situation may seem different to you. Reengage your head (your reason, logic, and intellect) and note how your thoughts about your circumstances may have changed. Have

confidence that you will make the "right" choices; continue to feel centered, knowing that you are not alone; be in touch with the needs of others around you in your situation; feel how your inner spirituality wants to express itself in your actions.

5. *Action:* Begin your action, make your decision, and face your situation. Know that this process of centering will help you in what will happen next. Stay with the present moment and trust that your inner process has led you to the best possible place from which you can draw on all your resources—your intellect, your emotions, and your body, including your voice and your body language. Have faith that you will respond to the situation and choose your path from your whole self and with your spirit connected to an ultimate goal and purpose.

6. *Compassion:* Be ready to forgive yourself. If you act and the results fall short of your expectations, or those of others, have compassion for yourself and others. As long as you live, there will be more opportunities to practice being a spiritual leader, a human being just like all of us. Know that if you make a mistake with the intent of doing good—if you engage with this task in a spirit of humility, and in touch with your higher purpose—all will be well.

READING LIST

If you wish to read more about Personal Growth and spiritual practices, consult the works listed in the References section below, or choose one from this list of some of my favorite books.

Au, W., & Cannon, N. (1995). *Urgings of the heart: A spirituality of integration.* New York: Paulist Press.

Bolman, L. G., & Deal, T. E. (1995). *Leading with soul: An uncommon journey of spirit.* San Francisco: Jossey-Bass.

Brantley, J. (2003). *Calming your anxious mind.* Oakland, CA: New Harbinger Publications.

Briskin, A. (1996). *The stirring of soul in the workplace.* San Francisco: Jossey-Bass.

(Continued)

(Continued)

Chopra, D. (1994). *The seven spiritual laws of success: A practical guide to the fulfillment of your dreams.* San Rafael, CA: Amber-Allen/New World Library.

Conger, J. A. (1998). *Spirit at work: Discovering the spirituality in leadership.* San Francisco: Jossey-Bass.

Covey, S. R. (1989). *The seven habits of highly effective people.* New York: Simon & Schuster.

Jaworski, J. (1998). *Synchronicity: The inner path of leadership.* San Francisco: Berrett-Koehler.

Kabat-Zinn, J. (1994). *Wherever you go, there you are: Mindfulness meditation in everyday life.* New York: Hyperion Books.

Keating, T. (1997). *Open mind, open heart.* New York: Continuum.

Koestenbaum, P. (2002). *Leadership: The inner side of greatness: A philosophy for leaders.* San Francisco: Jossey-Bass.

Kundtz, D. (2000). *Everyday serenity: Meditations for people who do too much.* New York: MJF Books.

Nhat Hanh, Thich (1976). *The miracle of mindfulness: A manual on meditation.* Boston: Beacon Press.

Thompson, C. M. (2000). *The congruent life: Following the inward path to fulfilling work and inspired leadership.* San Francisco: Jossey-Bass.

Tolle, E. (1999). *The power of now.* Novato, CA: New World Library.

Walsh, R. (1999). *Essential spirituality: The 7 central practices to awaken heart and mind.* New York: Wiley.

References

Covey, S. (2004). *The eighth habit: From effectiveness to greatness.* New York: Free Press.

Houston, P. D., & Sokolow, S. L. (2006). *The spiritual dimensions of leadership.* Thousand Oaks, CA: Corwin Press.

Metzger, C. (2006). *Balancing leadership and personal growth.* Thousand Oaks, CA: Corwin Press.

Moore, T. (1992). *Care of the soul: A guide for cultivating depth and sacredness in everyday life.* New York: Harper Perennial.

Moore, T. (2006, November/December). The spirituality in leadership. *Spirituality and health: The soul/body connection, 9*(6), 10–11.

CHAPTER EIGHT

SPIRITUALLY ORIENTED LEADERSHIP IN A SECULAR AGE

CHUCK BONNER

We are living in a secular age. Today the way of thinking that holds sway is cost-efficient, instrumental reasoning. Decisions are made based on the bottom line, on results and costs. This binary type of reasoning works well in dealing with business and technology, or in solving mathematical problems and disaggregating data. It is this type of cool, detached reasoning that can analyze the benefits of corporate downsizing and then justify it on the basis of its cost-efficiency. Not coincidentally, this same reasoning is at the core of No Child Left Behind (NCLB).

Now there is nothing inherently wrong with instrumental reasoning; it is not inherently subject to illogical or factual errors. However, what it does *not* do well is take into account human potential. Human potential is miraculous—nonsequential and hard to quantify. As an assistant principal, I see small miracles arising from human potential all the time. I see students who have failed every test they could possibly fail, and yet they walk in one day and somehow a light inside has suddenly gone on. How? Who knows? Events in their life have somehow clicked, and they are now willing to invest the work and effort to succeed. Or the student who has struggled with drugs and alcohol and is rapidly on the way to dropping out—and yet somehow is able to turn everything around and succeed. Or that large group of C-average students who somehow go on to do well in life. Or the learning-disabled students whose true abilities often don't show up in school—let alone on the narrow criteria of NCLB. Once those narrow criteria are no longer the only measure of their success, these kids also shine.

I don't know why all of these phenomena occur, but they usually have something to do with an adult who refused to give up on a child, who saw that child as more than his or her last test score. As more than a number.

Here's my point: These myriad small miracles are the kids who, in my mind, make up a large percentage of the children in our public schools. Understanding them requires a broader definition of what it is to be human than instrumental reasoning will allow. They may look poor quantitatively, but they shine qualitatively. In order to be able to shine qualitatively, however, a student must be *known* by a teacher or counselor or some other adult; some adult must recognize special qualities in a student, validating that young person.

I believe that the answer lies in spiritually oriented leadership—a style of leadership that embraces the whole student and sees the grave danger of overemphasizing cost-efficient thinking in education.

I fear that our current mode of thinking is keeping us from appreciating these kinds of hidden qualities in young people. We can justify corporate downsizing without much moral outrage. Events such as the ethical crimes at Enron and Unisys upset us for a bit, but we chalk it up to being the way of the world. And now, for similar reasons, we are embracing a rather dehumanized—and dehumanizing—form of schooling. I am coming to believe, though, that all participants in education are beginning to question our current approach. And I also believe that the answer lies in spiritually oriented leadership—a style of leadership that embraces the whole student and sees the grave danger of overemphasizing cost-efficient thinking in education.

A spiritually oriented leader seeks more than just quantitative change, such as higher scores on standardized tests. Higher scores can be achieved relatively easily (though not necessarily honestly). It is not difficult to focus on one indicator of success, teach accordingly, and hit the mark on that indicator. If you don't hit the mark the first time—well, you can always drop social studies from the curriculum and spend more time on what is being tested. That's absurd, you may say, reading it here in black and white, but it is happening. Drop an integral part of education simply to get a higher test score? Yes, it's happening in our schools. Someone somewhere must think it's an acceptable solution.

This type of thinking has come to pervade education. All the different views from all the different stakeholders on what education is or should be are left at the door of the public schools. And we are charged with making them work. It's no wonder that educators at all levels feel such enormous frustration. It is in our schools where all of society's disparate views on education impact our students; it is here where they get a name and a face.

For me this makes a huge difference. I am not dealing with a concept or an abstraction; I am seeing every day the impact on *people I know*—students, teachers, parents. I am dealing with kids who behave like kids, parents who love their kids and want the best for them, and teachers who want to see them succeed. To put the finest point on this, I am dealing with *people*—people who entrust their children to me, who trust that I am paying attention to what is happening to their children when they are in my charge. I find myself, these days, in a perpetual moral dilemma. I don't believe we can think about education properly when we limit ourselves to instrumental reasoning. The task of educating children has a moral component, and we have been trying to answer moral questions by using a form of reason not equipped for that purpose.

In recent years, the goal of education has been to score well on standardized tests; it is now the law. And because it is the law, these tests have become *high-stakes* tests. Graduation is based on these tests, teachers' and administrators' jobs are based on these tests, and schools can be taken over by the government based on these same tests. The stakes are truly high. But questions are beginning to arise from parents and school board members about the worthiness of NCLB. I believe we have a role in helping these stakeholders understand the true goals of education, what an educational leader is, and the place of spirituality in our secular world.

Education, Leaders, and Spirituality

Education is a difficult topic to write about. Everyone has a strong opinion about education, and it seems you really don't need to know anything about education to have one. We hear calls for more money for schooling, as well as warnings about throwing good money after bad. We hear warnings against the culture of testing, yet despite these warnings we see the steady implementation of more testing. There are federally mandated programs without funding, and the funding of mandated programs with funds from programs that have been eliminated. There are so many differing versions of the truth: from Republicans, from Democrats, and from progressives, traditionalists, alternativists, charterists, and cyberists—all proclaiming how they will meet every need of everyone.

Everyone has a strong opinion about education, and it seems you really don't need to know anything about education to have one.

Whose version of the truth is right, and how are we to decide? Maybe experts can help, but maybe not. The momentous *Nation at Risk* report, for instance, issued in 1983, has more recently been called flawed and misleading. Different studies from different think tanks report different conclusions on whether we are doing better or worse in educating our children. Whom do you believe? And who is accountable?

Accountability is an interesting question in itself, considering the structure of U.S. education. Teachers are hired by building administrators, who in turn are hired by district office administrators. District office administrators are hired by school boards, and school board members are elected by the community. Who's at the top of the educational ladder, and who's at the bottom? As far as hiring goes, it seems that the community, who elects the school board, is at the top. In terms of who is first to be fired, teachers would be at the bottom, followed by administrators.

But there's more to it than that, of course. Ironically, those same teachers and administrators who are first to be fired are also required to have more education. Teachers are required to be highly qualified on standardized tests given by the state in order to keep their jobs Teachers are expected to earn master's degrees (also a requirement for administrators), and it is recommended that administrators earn doctorates. No such recommendations are made for school boards or the community. In fact, school board members and members of the community are not required to have any knowledge of education at all. Those least educated about education are at the top of the heap.

Yet community members generally feel completely powerless at the hands of the school district, and school board members often feel at a loss as to how to keep the community happy. They, too, are conflicted about the multiple versions of education mentioned above. District office administrators are working hard to implement costly federal laws without raising the taxes of a community that is generally made up of a majority of people who have no children in school! Building-level administrators are trying to work everything into the curriculum and the schedule and have the schedule covered by teachers—all without assigning any more time or teachers to accomplish this gargantuan task. And teachers merely need to make all students in the United States—no matter what their ability or disability, emotional stability, socioeconomic situation, parental support or lack thereof, whether they speak English or not, or any of the countless issues that occur in a young person's life—proficient on a specific test, on a specific day. This in turn will tell us if the student can graduate, if the teacher is any good, if the school district is any good, and if the building administrators are any good.

Oddly enough, at this point the chain of accountability begins to break down. District administrators can be reprimanded, but they can always point to the teachers and building-level administrators as the real problem. The school board seems not to be in the accountability equation, nor is the community—and even the students are somehow able to blame the school for their failing and in some instances even get a voucher to go elsewhere. Least accountable of all are the lawyers or politicians who now play integral roles in public school education, for now we are back to the broad strokes of whether public education is in the dismal shape reported in the newspapers, which is based on the many different versions of what education is in the first place.

Whew!

To this conflicting and bewildering mix of perspectives we add the role of leadership. You'll admit that it may seem difficult to discern who is leading and who is accountable. So let me keep this close to home: with me. From my admittedly limited perspective as an assistant principal, I am unaware of the warring intentions of this vast group of possible leaders. I have my opinions, but I can't know for sure. I know that personally I do not believe what some profess to believe wholeheartedly, and others are certainly free to disagree with my beliefs about schooling and testing and society and the purpose of education. Some like my style of leadership; others probably do not. I think I have valid reasons for what I believe about education, but so do others who believe differently. Yes, I could be described as a leader in education—a low-level leader, but a leader nonetheless. I have a title, but does that make me a leader? There are some excellent teachers in my building who are great leaders; they make my job easy. But they don't have the title of a leader, nor the authority that would come with the title. So are they leaders? On the other hand, I have no real input into what occurs in education, which would indicate that I'm really more of a manager.

When I think about all of this, I begin to wonder if the term "educational leader" is not an oxymoron, because most of us in the field of education tend to act as managers more than as leaders. Sure, we have our opinions on NCLB or IDEA (the Individuals with Disabilities Education Act), but our input is pretty limited. Some of us agree with these laws and others disagree, but we are far more the managers who carry out what the laws tell us to do than we are leaders. If we were to say no to the provisions of these laws, we would risk losing our jobs and incur the loss of federal funds needed to run the schools. If you are a district administrator, you have sworn an oath to uphold the laws. You would be in a rather awkward position if you chose to defy the law after having sworn to uphold it.

Therefore, from my admittedly limited point of view, the issue of leadership is also conflicted.

Now we add to this interesting mix the notion of *spiritually oriented* leadership. What is that anyway? Do we consider the leaders of the country we are currently at war with to be spiritual? Are the leaders of our country who claim to be spiritual, actually spiritual? Certainly the followers of each set of leaders—those who care about such things, anyway—believe their leaders to be spiritual.

Some of us are confident that we can define what it means to us to be spiritual. Others could provide a pretty good argument that there's no such thing as spirituality! You could probably supply many proofs and dis-proofs of your own; after all, the argument about spirituality has been going on for centuries. That's interesting in itself, of course—that we've not been able to answer conclusively what "spiritual" is—nor what leadership is, nor for that matter what education is. Hmmm. . . .

Education can open up whole new worlds, but it can also be employed to indoctrinate and to close minds. Which version of education do you prefer? As for leadership, Hitler was certainly a leader, and so was Gandhi. Each had his share of zealous followers. Personally, I like Gandhi's version of leadership. As to spirituality, well, consider Jim Jones (whose disciples in the Peoples Temple committed mass suicide) and Martin Luther King, Jr., both of whom also had zealous followers. Personally, I like the King version. How about you?

I'm using extreme examples, you may say. I agree, but every leader in between those extremes falls somewhere along that spectrum. Let me be clear: I am *not* suggesting that anyone is a Hitler or a Gandhi. Please understand that. I *am* suggesting that Hitler and

Our everyday decisions may seem small and insignificant, but I maintain that our decisions reveal us: what we are willing to commit ourselves to, our tendencies, and our values.

Gandhi mark the extreme ends of a continuum—and that our own decisions direct us toward one end or the other. At the time, our everyday decisions may seem small and insignificant, but I maintain that our decisions reveal us: what we are willing to commit ourselves to, our tendencies, and our values.

I believe that we know the differences between a Hitler and a Gandhi. I believe, too, that the followers of a Hitler are persuaded by a smaller, more limited, easier truth—one that requires much less thinking on the follower's part. The followers of a Gandhi are persuaded by a larger, universal, more difficult truth—one that requires a large intellectual and moral commitment on the part of the follower. The truths of a Hitler tend to divide us from one another; the truths of a Gandhi tend to unify. Hitler saw the Jews as a problem; his solution was to annihilate them. Gandhi, I suspect, would have suggested that, if you see others as a problem, the answer is to love them even more. Hitler was prepared to sacrifice those who were not in accord with his beliefs, with his worldview. Gandhi was absolutely prepared to sacrifice himself so that others might fare better.

This seems to me to be the litmus test for whether spiritually oriented leadership is at work: division and exclusion versus loving, embracing inclusion; punitive and self-serving versus loving and self-sacrificing.

Where are you as an administrator? Do you find yourself questioning the moral implications of your decisions? Does your conscience ever tug at you in your everyday life as an administrator? Mine tugs at me a lot. I question a lot. Change in schools—and far beyond schools, too—comes at the cost of the status quo. I don't think I'm all that different from the average educator. I expect that we all find ourselves switching back and forth in small ways from the smaller, more limited, easier truth, which requires much less thinking on our part, to the larger, universal, more difficult truth, which requires a large intellectual commitment on our part. We all do it. We are all doing our best to justify our decisions, worrying about doing the right thing for kids—and worrying, too, about doing the right thing to keep our job. Life as an educator is a moral dilemma.

So, using the simple scale I just proposed, what do I see going on in education from my assistant principal's desk? From my perspective, it appears that we base many of our decisions on cost-efficient thinking. This type of thinking is not, unfortunately, very helpful in achieving Gandhi-like goals. The Gandhi part of us asks that we love more—love the enemy, love each other. Gandhi would want us to be in win-win situations. Gandhi-like thinking is not cost-efficient, not oriented to short-term solutions. If Gandhi were a superintendent, his budget would probably be a mess, and he would not go along with that which he did not believe. And he probably wouldn't last long in public education. (For that matter, Jesus would have loved all the kids in detention; he would probably have been removed from administration and put into counseling.)

Ironically, the opposite approach can be very efficient in the short term. As an extreme example, Hitler chose to eliminate what was standing in his way. Surprisingly, the thinking that informed his approach is not dissimilar to that involved in corporate downsizing: the elimination of people for the benefit of the company. Consider how objectified and dehumanized Hitler made the Jewish people; he was able to turn them into a list of tattooed numbers. If you are able to reduce people to numbers, their elimination—or at least their manipulation—seems much more palatable. It can seem immoral to cut off people's financial well-being in the name of corporate downsizing, but sadly that behavior is accepted as the cost of doing business. Whether then or now, that kind of instrumental, cost-efficient thinking does not require moral calculations. Win-win decisions are more difficult to make than win–lose decisions.

From my perspective, short-term, cost-efficient, punitive modes of thinking are not helpful in any way when dealing with children.

I cannot get around this conclusion. If we base our decisions on cost-efficiency, can the results of those decisions be in the best interests of children? I think not. Very simply put, if I base my decisions about your child on costs, my allegiance is to something other than your child. Am I being idealistic and naïve? After all, we live in a capitalistic society, right? And we are children of our times. In a capitalistic society, our default mode of thinking is cost-efficiency. Nevertheless, if we are to think morally, we must reset our default away from cost-efficient thinking.

I attend many parent meetings, and I talk with parents every day. I hear how wonderfully we are doing, and I hear things that would burn off your ears. The most difficult meeting for me is when I bump up against that cost-efficient, business-oriented part of school that I see as harmful to children. Most painful for me is when it's my job to implement or enforce a rule or policy—and when my conscience goes against such an action. Imagine having to explain to a parent that his or her child did not meet the requirements of IDEA because the child's lower IQ and low grades did not indicate a learning disability, and therefore did not permit the child to qualify for services under IDEA. Some parents respond to this by saying, "Then, according to your formula, if he does start to fail, he would qualify?" This is not a comfortable conversation. What do you say to parents whose kid has fallen through the cracks in the system? Here's a paradox for you: according to IDEA, children learn differently; according to NCLB, children test the same. Even the laws we must enforce are in conflict—and our children are trapped in the middle.

Teachers and administrators are caught in the middle in a different way. We need to think cost-efficiently to fit students into programs and schedules and to be able to pay for them, yet we must also think morally about what is best for the student. Many times what we are asked to do places us in conflict, and yet we must explain to the

> *Here is the heart of the dilemma: We all have to survive in a secular, money-driven world that runs on cost-efficient thinking. Yet our children simply cannot be comprehended in terms of cost-efficient thinking.*

parent why the cost-efficient answer is the best for his or her child—*or* we go out on a limb and support the parent at what may be our own expense. Educators sit smack in the middle: wanting to do everything for the children in our charge, so long as it does not cost any money or raise taxes.

Here is the heart of the dilemma: *We all have to survive in a secular, money-driven world that runs on cost-efficient thinking.* Yet our children simply cannot be comprehended in terms of cost-efficient thinking; only a moral or spiritual way of thinking can come close to capturing the way we think (and feel) about our children. So how does an administrator navigate these two divergent modes of thinking? How do we do what is morally right at bargain-basement prices?

MORAL OBLIGATION IN A COST-EFFICIENT WORLD

When looking at the effects of NCLB, we tend to think in terms of the context we are currently working in, and thus we limit our perspective. Some administrators have gone through school takeovers and the firing of teachers and administrators. Some are working in districts that are part public schools and part for-profit schools. Some work in buildings surrounded by abject poverty, some are in wealthy districts, and some are in between. Each has different problems related to educating children.

Part of my job according to NCLB is to make Adequate Yearly Progress (AYP) as defined by high-stakes, standardized testing. Not making AYP in successive years can cause teachers and administrators to lose their jobs and the school to be taken over by the state. Now it's true that a number of studies have indicated that socioeconomic status alone is a better indicator of future academic success than any standardized test. Studies have also indicated that whites perform better on standardized tests than do many minorities. This suggests that an administrator working in an impoverished, mostly minority district is on a different playing field from one working in a wealthy district. On yet another playing field would be an administrator working in a district with a large number of non–English-speaking students. My point is that while the test is standardized, the participants are not.

Let's imagine a district that seemingly has it all: a high proportion of both white students and wealth, remediation opportunities built into the schedule, successive years of students scoring either perfect scores on SATs or in the 2300s, and a large number of parents with college degrees. You might think that this district would not suffer some of the punitive ramifications of NCLB. However, other schools in the area have been taken over. Some have been privatized. Some have dropped social studies in order to spend more time on math and English—the two subjects by which we are judged as succeeding or failing.

Now let me go back to our simple test: Will I base my decisions on punitive, self-serving, cost-efficient thinking, or on the constant messy questioning of what is best for all children? Where do I stand on a law that is not affecting me yet, but is in my opinion adversely affecting surrounding schools and districts? Where do I stand on NCLB if I base my reaction on how it affects only me, in my district alone? If I choose not to speak out because I am currently not affected, then it would seem that I am in accord with a law that is adversely affecting neighboring districts. What if, using us-and-them thinking, I ignore children in those other districts, whose students suffer the effects of obstacles that my kids may never even know about?

Come on, you might protest. Most of us have enough problems facing us without tackling the problems of other districts. Okay, but could we make our own community aware of the overall impact of NCLB on *all* children, not just our own? Morally, I think we need to do just that. We may be looked at rather oddly, but we should encourage conversations that look beyond our own little piece of the world. Here is a very subtle test of which way we are leaning: are we limiting our concern only to our kids, our taxes, our backyard—or are we taking into account the whole messy issue of how this law is affecting *all* of America's children.

Testing

A large chunk of NCLB is concerned with testing. Most people involved in education have a limited understanding of testing, especially high-stakes testing. Developing accurate, valid test questions is in itself very difficult. The norming and standardization of such tests is also a lengthy, difficult process. Even less understood, though, is what standardized tests are developed to *do*.

Standardized tests are developed to rank students, to spread them out across a scale. To accomplish this, there must be a cutoff score—above which the student is ranked proficient, and below which a student is ranked not proficient. The cut scores we currently use are arbitrary, and the cutoff level is raised each year to another arbitrary level. Why, for example, is it determined that a score of 200 is *not* proficient but a 201 *is*?

NCLB charges educators with making every student proficient on a standardized test by the year 2014. (The selection of 2014 and not 2013 or 2015 is also arbitrary.) We are to do that by way of an indicator that is designed to rank students from high to low. In essence, using our current indicator we will never reach proficiency because the test is designed to rank students above and below the arbitrary cut score. One could argue that if the tests are criterion-referenced rather than norm-referenced, all students could potentially be above the cut score. But this assumes that all students are on the same playing field—and we know that they are not. Both students and schools are ranked by this arbitrary and rather incoherent method.

More to the point, students lose opportunities and educators can lose their jobs based on these same scores. *Public education as a whole is being judged exclusively on a test designed to not allow it to succeed* And when those arbitrary scores are published in the newspapers, we as a society see them as the "facts" proving that public education is failing. How can this be? Well, for some reason we are willing to believe that those furthest from the actual business of interacting with children—those politicians and test makers and think tank pundits—are in fact experts on education. We are caught up in a perfect example of cost-efficient thinking: the quantification of our children by means of test scores.

As an assistant principal, I have nearly given up this fight. To raise this issue is to be immediately marginalized. Here is the power of cost-efficient thinking at work. Think of my simple scale above: Are my decisions based on punitive, self-serving, cost-efficient, binary thinking, or are they based on the constant, messy questioning of what is best for all children? Testing of the sort mandated by NCLB is not formative; it does not add to the student's learning in any way. The test arbitrarily sorts students into those who pass and those who fail. The repercussions are punitive in that this test, and this test alone, decides whether or not a student graduates. Therefore, rather than entering into time-consuming, messy human relationships in order to know students and their situations, we can test four or five hundred students at a pop for several hours and know with certainty (or so we believe) whether those students are fit to move on.

In the final analysis, why this system is the way it is both eludes and frightens me. How people can morally accept this way of dealing with and categorizing students scares me to death. A single test from somewhere far away designed to rank students by means of an arbitrary cutoff score is being used to define our children as proficient or not—and we say okay.

Imagine explaining that to a parent whose child did not meet the arbitrary cutoff score and is now in danger of not graduating. Imagine further that you *know* this student and parent. You know that he is a hard worker, an excellent kid, an A/B student. Now imagine explaining that, because he did not pass the standardized test, he cannot take some of the elective classes he had planned to take because he must

We are caught up in a perfect example of cost-efficient thinking: the quantification of our children by means of test scores.

be put in a remedial local assessment class. Are we truly helping this student by removing him from senior electives? Most surprising to me is that this process is seldom questioned by parents, or even by board members. Even as I raise this issue, I am aware that I risk looking at best naïve, and at worst just plain silly.

Testing and Scheduling

The high-stakes testing machine also affects scheduling. Students who fail the test must then be assigned to local assessment classes for their senior year. This requires that they be removed from elective classes. Running elective classes requires having a set minimum number of students who sign up for that specific elective. If the class does not meet the minimum number, the class will not run. So if an elective class has a set minimum number of 12 and has, say, 15 students in it, and of those 15 students, 4 have failed the Pennsylvania System of School Assessment (PSSA), the class will not run. So not only does the testing affect the 4 students who failed the test, but it also affects the 11 who can no longer take the class because it will not be offered. In this scenario, even students who do well on the PSSA are punished.

Another fallout from this situation is that there must be a teacher to teach the local assessment class. This teacher must be pulled from another class. The more students who fail the PSSA, the more teachers must be pulled from other classes. The result is fewer classes for all students to choose from. So it's not just the student who fails the high-stakes test who is affected by NCLB—it's all students. Individual student schedules, teacher schedules, and even the master schedule are built around the demands of NCLB.

Testing and Teacher Hiring

This type of testing is also beginning to govern the hiring of teachers. According to NCLB, teachers must score as "highly qualified" on standardized tests in order to keep their jobs. Most teachers can achieve this goal. I have noticed, however, that such a test does not help identify someone who can teach! It merely identifies someone who possesses content knowledge.

Let me ask you a question. Do you remember a teacher back in high school or college who may have been highly intelligent, but when you left his or her class it didn't feel as if any of the teacher's knowledge made it out of the person's head and into yours? On the other hand, do you remember that teacher whose class you were reluctant to leave because you were so engaged in the subject? As an administrator who is part of the hiring process, I cannot tell which kind of teacher I'm getting when I review the paperwork and stamp Teacher X as "highly qualified."

A question I always ask a prospective teacher is, "What do you do as a new teacher in the building when in the first week of school a student in your class speaks in a vulgar and inappropriate way? How do you get that student back into the fold to have a productive year?" Some candidates say right away that they would follow whatever the disciplinary code demands. That answer is certainly appropriate. Or they may recommend sending the student to the guidance counselor to see if an outside issue might be bothering the student. Again appropriate. But then there are those whose immediate response is to talk with the student to see what is wrong; some even say they would check to see if they themselves had said something to cause the behavior. Think of our simple scale again. The first two candidates have, to some degree, removed themselves from the situation by following school rules and by using guidance services; the third assumes the responsibility of trying to build a relationship. In which direction on our scale might these different candidates be leaning? What indication do I receive of what type of teacher they will be?

I have a zillion tales of teachers who did not fare well on standardized tests, and who did not even interview well, but who were absolutely phenomenal with students and parents. You know the ones I'm talking about. They are at every dance, at games on Saturday, involved in all types of events. In our current test-dominated system, some of these people never get past the paper review. We look at their scores on paper. All of them who don't hit the mark are eliminated. They could have been phenomenal, but they never get a chance—just like some of our students.

And there's more: According to NCLB, I now have to find special education teachers who are highly qualified in several content areas in order to be allowed to teach special education. How many certified special education teachers do you know who are certified in special education and also in two other areas: mathematics, science, English, or social studies? Considering all the litigation that special education teachers are currently involved in concerning the conflicts between NCLB and IDEA, this is yet another obstacle they must hurdle. And, of course, in order for a special education teacher to become certified in these areas, he or she must pass a battery of standardized tests. As important as caring relationships between teachers and students always are, they are doubly important for special education teachers and their students. Yet our current criteria for hiring and retaining teachers does nothing to assess those kinds of relational, people skills that are essential for developing a love of learning in children.

Not surprisingly, one commission looking into the reauthorization of NCLB is suggesting that building principals must also pass a test to show that they have the skills to be effective leaders. Most disconcerting in all of this testing is that the vast majority of the people making such suggestions have never been involved in the teaching profession or passed one test required to become a teacher. Yet Senate hearings are convened to listen to suggestions from Bill Gates for improving education! How did Mr. Gates become an expert in education?

Students are tested. Teachers are tested. Some are urging that principals be tested. All of these tests come with serious consequences. There is a significant conflict here, as we in education are expected to create a love of learning by way of punitive, federally mandated testing.

Testing appears to be here to stay, however. Secretary of Education Margaret Spellings is calling for more testing in the form of Graduate Competence Assessments. The aim, I suppose, is to make the teaching profession teacher-proof. If you believe that teachers are doing a terrible job, then this is a good thing. If you believe that teachers become teachers because they want to help students learn and grow, then this is a sad time in the history of our profession. According to our simple scale, which way are you leaning?

Now you might be feeling—as some policy makers obviously are—that all of this testing is necessary because students aren't learning, teachers aren't teaching, and administrators aren't administrating properly, but where do we get this perspective? I know of no teachers who, when they were in high school, decided on teaching as a career because they saw it as a path on which they could hurt the most children. I know of no teachers who entered the profession with the goal of making students' learning experiences miserable.

Yet consider the media coverage about education since the *Nation at Risk* report more than 20 years ago. We have heard it constantly: We are failing! And we have been in this terrible situation for quite some time. What I cannot understand is how we who have been educated in public schools during these years of dismal education are now able to critique public education. Shouldn't we all be too uneducated to know any better? Even more ironic, though, we have been increasing the use of testing in an effort to solve this problem for roughly 40 years—and yet, according to those same tests, we are still failing. We are forced to implement more and more testing, and still we fail! So the experts tell us to test some more.

Why do we accept this? How do we as leaders justify our actions? All of public education is now geared toward testing and the effects of testing. Testing begins in third grade and continues through eighth grade, and then picks up again in eleventh grade. If a student does not score at a proficient level in eleventh grade, then that student will be retested in twelfth grade. We spend an appalling amount of time and money on testing our children.

On the other hand, what if our job were construed as helping young people to leave our care able to "deal in a flexible and successful way with the problems of life and of eternity" (Quigley, 1966)? What are we doing to help students with this most fundamental aspect of life? Do we not owe the children we work with at least this much? If we do not embrace the model of spiritually oriented leadership—the only model with the power to bring both teachers and students to full humanness; to full creativity; and to being fully alive physically, mentally, emotionally, and spiritually—then we are creating partial people who can only lead partial lives.

If we were living during the Industrial Revolution, this type of testing for fragmented bits of knowledge might suffice, but today this type of sequential learning is completely inadequate to our students' future needs. What students are learning this year can by next year be outdated.

The whole process of education is being questioned—and rightfully so. Cyberschools are the fastest-growing schools in America. The entire sequential notion of K–12 education is being rethought, and when and where students learn is now an open question.

We are in a time of rapid advances, global development, and cultural conflict—all happening at a pace never seen before. Right now, the majority of information we test for can be found on the Internet in seconds. Do we need to teach writing skills and mathematics? Absolutely! But what is more essential is that we teach those skills by using creative, imaginative processes.

At the building level, all the policies and laws and tests happen to real people—people I know. They happen to people who trust me with their children.

Today's students will reach young adulthood facing a job market that has yet to be created. They will be working with people from all around the world. While the three R's are still important, we should be teaching our young people to *think*—not just to recall facts. Our student will need to imagine and put together information in new ways.

In my current job, we are attempting to accomplish this task in a number of ways. We have a project in partnership with a local hotel that allows students to become actively engaged in the business end of creating a banquet for over 300 people. They need to raise money, advertise, interview for jobs, organize, and staff the affair. While doing all of these tasks, they have to fulfill the academic pieces involved in finance, business, and management.

We are also involved with an exchange program with a school in Denmark. Danish students come to our school and live with our families for about 10 days, and then our students visit Denmark to do the same. Some of the relationships developed in this program have been maintained for several years.

Think of the people skills, the real-world experience, the learning about different cultures that is happening in these and other such programs. Imagine the thinking skills required to accommodate all that goes on to set up a functioning banquet or a program of international travel. Unfortunately, these programs do not lend themselves to testing, as is true of most of real life. So why must we test everyone at every turn? Many schools have lost their art and shop programs; some have even lost social studies. I fear that, in time, we may lose the programs I just mentioned.

CONCLUSION

My daughter Olivia will begin kindergarten next year. She will graduate from high school in 2020. As a loving father, and as a professional educator, I have many concerns as to what she will encounter in her public school experience. Will she get to experience those teachable moments when a teacher can follow the students' interests? Those moments are being lost. Teacher autonomy is being lost. Or will she encounter only an ever-growing battery of tests administered in a punitive culture?

I have seen teachers overcome just about all odds: overcrowded and underfunded classrooms, insufficient supplies, as well as a great many problems caused by larger problems in our society. I find myself imagining what these dedicated and overstressed teachers could accomplish if they were not constrained by law and policies that seem to me to be designed to undermine and sabotage their best work.

Educational leaders should be questioning what the politicians have created. I do not believe I am saying anything that most people do not already believe. But I believe there is a fear of speaking out. If we consider the spiritually oriented leaders I discussed earlier (Gandhi and Dr. King), it's useful to remember that they're not living in the Hamptons and enjoying lucrative retirement packages. They were both killed. I am not advocating that you place yourself in such jeopardy, but our voices must be heard! No, speaking out will not make cost-efficient sense, and we are not likely to skyrocket to educational fame and fortune. In fact, the opposite is more likely. But we are morally obligated to follow the still small voice of our conscience. Only in so doing will others begin to question what we as a society are doing to our children.

At the building level, all the policies and laws and tests happen to real people—people I know. They happen to people who trust me with their children. It is impossible to gain the trust of people without being honest. And there's no doubt that dealing honestly with people can be messy.

If we wish to see true reform, we must cultivate spiritually oriented leaders in all aspects of public life. To accomplish this, there must be spiritual leadership within public education. If this is to happen—and I believe that it *must* happen—there needs to be a change in public education, and I think the change needs to come from within ourselves. We need to access a part of ourselves that questions the structures that are currently forcing us into decisions about children that may not be best for those children or for the future of our society. And we need to start now.

REFERENCES

National Commission on Excellence in Education. (1983). *A nation at risk: The imperative for educational reform.* Washington, DC: U.S. Department of Education.

Quigley, C. (1966). *Tragedy and hope: A history of the world in our time.* New York: MacMillan.

CHAPTER NINE

SPIRITUAL LEADERSHIP— THE INVISIBLE REVOLUTION

SCOTT THOMPSON

Today's prevailing materialistic culture tells a story of life and leadership that's about staying in control, gaining and maintaining political advantage, and enlarging one's status and material wealth. The mentality engendered by the culture of materialism would tend to dismiss any so-called spiritual dimension. Or, even when the possibility of spirituality is tacitly acknowledged, it is still kept at a "prudent distance" from things professional.

In education, school and district leaders work in environments that are socially, politically, and structurally complex. The demands of successfully—or even acceptably—navigating this territory are immense. A leader must be keenly aware of what's going on around him or her and be able to take effective action when circumstances call for it. A superintendent, for example, needs to be attuned to developments and dynamics concerning the school board, cabinet and other central office administrators and staff members, schools, parents, community, and local political leadership—all the while operating within the confines of state and national policy frameworks.

So the obvious story of educational leadership in the first decade of the 21st century is very much about mastering the externals. There is, however, a strikingly different (though far less pervasive) story. Hidden as this other story tends to be, it is in fact revolutionary in its dimension and potential. It's what we might call the inside story—the inner world of individual leaders. This story is about heart and consciousness and spirituality. It is in no way isolated from the very real external demands that leaders must tackle. It is not about separation—a sealed-off inner world blissfully free from all that "real" leaders must grapple with. This story of leadership is not about fragmentation, but rather wholeness. It's about bringing the whole self, including spiritual resources, to bear on the tangible problems that leaders must face in the complicated world of schools and districts As Margaret Wheatley (2005) has noted, "leadership today is spiritual" (p. x).

SPIRITUAL LEADERSHIP

What is spiritual leadership? And what is *not* spiritual leadership?

My short definition of spiritual leadership goes like this: *Spirituality* is a state of mind or consciousness that enables one to perceive deeper levels of experience, meaning, values, and purpose than can be perceived from a strictly materialistic vantage point. *Spiritual leadership,* then, is leading from those deeper levels (Thompson, 2005b, p. 5).

> *Spiritual leadership is not about slipping religion back into classrooms, district offices, or the room where the school board meets.*

Spiritual leadership is *not* about slipping religion back into classrooms, district offices, or the room where the school board meets. While spiritual leadership for some may be rooted in particular religious traditions, it's important that public school leaders not engage in sectarian proselytizing or speech that can have the effect of "establishing" a particular religious persuasion in a publicly "owned" institution.

As important as I believe it is to respect and uphold the wall of separation between church and state, it is also vitally important for leaders not to internalize that wall in such a way that they seal off their own spiritual resources and end up bringing only a portion of who they are to their work in the secular world of public education.

"The search for meaning, purpose, wholeness, and integration is a constant, never-ending task," writes Fred Stokley (2002), a retired public school district superintendent. "To confine this search to one day a week or after hours violates people's basic sense of integrity of being whole persons. In short, spirituality is not something one leaves at home" (p. 50).

So there we have a brief definition of spiritual leadership and a distinction from leadership that would foist religious particularities into school discourse. But what then are the dimensions of authentic spiritual leadership? From what I've learned so far, I believe they include the following:

- Moral leadership, grounded in moral purpose and moral passion;
- Servant-leadership;
- Leadership that promotes trust, openness, ownership, vision, and values;
- Distributing power rather than trying to willfully control it;
- Humility in leadership;
- Leading from inner peace and clarity even when faced with external storms; and
- Consciousness of the underlying wholeness of people and organizations.

Access to these dimensions, and the development of them, requires the exercise of spiritual practices or habits.

Moral Leadership

Educational leadership that is rooted in moral purpose and moral passion is indispensable; nothing less can answer the urgent need for sustainable progress. Each year of crawling, halting progress in public schools entails educational loss for lots and lots of children. When a child drops out or disengages or falls hopelessly behind, a blanket of darkness is cast over his or her future. When we consider the magnitude of this problem, we see also a stunting of our collective future.

Allison Phinney (2002) articulates the urgent need for change in terms that are broader than public education alone, but that speak powerfully to educational leaders:

Revolutionary change is needed. The ponderous pace of theory and debate is simply too slow to save humanness from being swallowed up in the opportunism of materialism, from being redefined, dispersed, swept away, unremembered. Now we need not so much the historian's late and sober assessment as the poet's, the dramatist's, the human being's passionate outrage and wakened alarm. More primary than each person's self-awareness of national or academic or professional identity—lawyer, economist, educator—must be a readiness to measure one's own consciousness of the human spirit against, not only terrible atrocity, but the equally terrible deadening of morality and spirit that leads to unchecked crimes against humanity and the loss of civilization. (p. 242)

We do need to directly and honestly face doggedly persistent achievement gaps that pervade our systems of public education. But that facing of facts needs to be accompanied by thoughtful, passionate, evidence-based action—action that is continuously informed by a commitment to the preciousness of our children.

We need moral purpose, a profound commitment to powerfully educate *all* of the children and young people in our care. That sense of purpose must ignite and feed the flames of moral outrage and passionate, unflagging leadership to bring justice and opportunity to children and young people who hold human destiny in their hearts and minds.

We need moral purpose, a profound commitment to powerfully educate all of the children and young people in our care.

It is not as though we simply need a few morally passionate souls in our midst, a passionate leader here and a passionate teacher there. Creating educational systems that powerfully serve the needs and potentials of all students cannot be done without widespread and sustained commitment fueled by moral passion and rooted in moral purpose.

"Passion is not an event," writes Derrick Bell (2002), "but an energy; and it's an energy that exists in all of us, all the time. The question is not whether we have it but whether we access it, and how we channel it" (pp. 23–24).

SERVANT-LEADERSHIP

The concept of leadership has sometimes evoked images of a charismatic or autocratic figure lording it over his or her followers, compelling them into compliance. Servant-leadership represents a dramatically different conception of leadership—one that consciously blurs the distinction between leadership and service. It aims not for compliance but for commitment, a joint ownership of the organization and its mission.

It was Robert Greenleaf who coined the term and developed the concept of "servant-leadership" with the publication in 1970 of an essay called *The Servant as Leader,* in which he wrote that servant-leadership

> begins with the natural feeling that one wants to serve, to serve first. Then conscious choice brings one to aspire to lead. The difference manifests itself in the care taken by the servant—first to make sure that other people's highest-priority needs are being served. The best test is: Do those served grow as persons; do they, while being served, become healthier, wiser, freer, more autonomous, more likely themselves to become servants? (as quoted in Spears, 1995, p. 4)

This idea certainly emerged from Greenleaf's own half-century of experience in the corporate world, but what directly triggered the paradoxical image of servant-leader was his response to reading a work of fiction by Herman Hesse called *Journey to the East.* Greenleaf summarizes the story:

> In this story we see a band of men on a mythical journey. . . . The central figure of the story is Leo, who accompanies the party as the servant who does the menial chores, but who also sustains them with his spirit and his song. He is a person of extraordinary presence. All goes well until Leo disappears. Then the group falls into disarray and the journey is abandoned. They cannot make it without the servant Leo. The narrator, one of the party, after some years of wandering, finds Leo and is taken into the Order that had sponsored the journey. There he discovers that Leo, whom he had known first as servant, was in

fact the titular head of the Order, its guiding spirit, a great and noble *leader.* (as quoted in Sergiovanni, 1992, p. 124)

This sense of service, existing at the heart of authentic leadership, is not only service to others, service to followers, but also service to a greater purpose and service to followers by helping them discover and be committed to the same greater purpose.

"Leading is giving. It is serving," according to Stokley (2002). "Leadership is an ethic—a gift of oneself to a common cause, a higher calling. . . . When their gifts are genuine and the spirit is right, their giving transforms a school or school district from a mere place of work to a shared way of life" (p. 50).

LEADERSHIP THAT PROMOTES A CULTURE OF TRUST, OPENNESS, AND OWNERSHIP, BUILT ON A FOUNDATION OF CORE VALUES

That a politicized, fear-based, excuse-prone, top-down culture is antithetical to sustainable high performance in public education is a no-brainer (Thompson, 2006, p. 44). It's also axiomatic that a culture of trust, openness, and collaboration built on shared ownership of core values and a compelling vision is crucial for sustaining high performance in public schools. What this means is that, unless an optimal culture for high performance is in place, reculturing must be at the core of the work of educational leadership.

Okay, but what *is* organizational culture? In essence, it is the underlying shared beliefs, history, assumptions, norms, and values that manifest themselves in patterns of behavior—or, in other words, "the way we do things around here." Reculturing, then, is fundamentally altering an organization's culture. Leaders of high-performing school systems train much of their strategic attention on reculturing, because that's where the mother lode of leverage for lasting change is located. *And that reculturing is spiritual work,* in that it is concerned with currents and dimensions that are not visible on the surface and that get at the heart of things.

A culture of trust, openness, and continuous improvement gives traction to large-scale reforms. It enables leaders and stakeholders to tap into and capitalize upon their collective potential. For large-scale improvement to take hold, connections are essential, and these connections are formed out of trust. Trust engenders openness, openness invites connections, and connections stimulate the inquiry and innovation that are essential to the creation of high-performing systems of schools—schools where all children are thriving in an atmosphere of high expectations and unwavering support.

We know that adaptability and flexibility are premium organizational capacities in today's environment of rapidly accelerating change. But where schools and school systems are not firmly anchored, high adaptability and flexibility lead to potentially destructive instability. An organization—any organization— that is unclear about its reason for being and consequently lurches from one fad or program to another is bound to become superfluous or dysfunctional.

A system of schools that is anchored in a set of core values—an immutable sense of purpose—is uniquely positioned to achieve foundational continuity despite changes in leadership.

Schools and districts, especially in urban areas, are prone to a procession of successive leaders, and often the appearance of a new superintendent or principal involves the unveiling of a new agenda based on a new vision or set of values. A system of schools that is anchored in a set of core values—an immutable sense of purpose— is uniquely positioned to achieve foundational continuity despite changes in leadership.

DISTRIBUTING POWER INSTEAD OF TRYING TO WILLFULLY CONTROL IT

Can a complex organization, such as a public school system, be controlled? I join many other observers and practitioners in concluding that the notion of controlling an organization or social system is either an illusion or the by-product of such a heavy-handed approach that all expressions of ingenuity, vision, openness, trust, ownership, and vitality become strangled. What the leaders then control is not a living institution but rather an organizational corpse.

Does a leader's facing up to the illusive nature of control necessarily have to be disempowering? Or can power be garnered in reaching *beyond* the illusion of control? If so, what sort of power? And what is a leader's role in relation to this power that lies beyond control?

What if our sense of power was not about competition for a scarce resource, but distribution from a limitless source? "Because power is energy, it needs to flow through organizations; it cannot be bounded or designated to certain functions or levels," writes Margaret Wheatley (1999). "What gives power its charge, positive or negative, is the nature of the relationship. When power is shared in such workplace designs as participative management and self-managed teams, positive creative power abounds" (p. 40). But when power is hoarded, manipulated, or selectively allocated on political grounds, creative energy is sucked out of the organization, and what fills the vacuum is politics as usual.

"Power isn't a piece of pie. The more power you give away, the more you have," says leadership consultant and former school principal John Morefield. "There isn't really a lot of institutional or positional power left in the principalship." The same goes for superintendents and their cabinet members and for union leaders and school board members. "But there is tremendous opportunity for referent power and moral authority—that kind of power that comes with building community" (as quoted in Thompson, 2005b, pp. 120–21).

The distribution of leadership is a way of marrying power to freedom. In such an environment, a superintendent's or principal's power is not diminished but enhanced. Instead of being a leader of followers, he or she is a leader of leaders. A genuine commitment to and thoughtful pursuit of this way of working is indispensable to developing the extent of shared ownership that whole-school and whole-system improvement requires. If we've awakened and discovered that we're living in a flat world, perhaps it is time to learn to lead our schools and districts horizontally.

HUMILITY IN LEADERSHIP

Great spiritual leaders in traditions throughout the world are distinguished by their humility. There's a simple explanation for the universality and indispensability of humility to powerful spiritual practice. A self-absorbed and overinflated human ego is not so adept at yielding to powers that are far greater than itself. Also, take a careful look at your own ego when it has become puffed up (yes, it happens to all of us from time to time). The ego, at such times, is stuffed with illusions. Its windows on what is spiritually possible are fogged by self-delusions. Humility, on the other hand, opens the doors and windows into a deeper experience of reality.

But is this talk of humility relevant to the sophisticated demands and complicated context faced by those who would lead schools and districts in the 21st century? It is indeed, and I base this conclusion on research, not just personal conviction.

Jim Collins and a research team of 20 graduate students spent 5 years researching the best-selling business book *Good to Great* (2001). Out of 1,435 companies, they found just 11 that met the good-to-great standard. After a period of performance somewhere in the good-to-mediocre range, these 11 companies broke through to greatness, meaning that they achieved market returns that at least tripled the returns of the general market for 15 straight years. Most of the thousands of hours of research and deliberation that Collins and his research associates devoted to this effort were spent trying to determine what distinguished these organizations from their peers—specifically, 11 comparison companies in the same industries that never rose to greatness.

Several counterintuitive essentials emerged, including that of "Level 5 leadership." All 11 good-to-great companies had Level 5 leaders, but none of the 11 comparison companies did. Level 5 leaders combine *personal humility* with what Collins (2001) describes as a "ferocious resolve, an almost stoic determination to do whatever needs to be done to make the company great" (p. 30). The Level 5 leader is powerfully focused on and committed to something larger than self-interest.

But can humility be developed? I believe that it can and that one way to do so is by going through spiritual experiences that enlarge one's sense of the powers and possibilities that extend beyond what a preoccupied human ego is able to perceive. This calls for disciplined practice.

Without intuition or spiritual sensing, there can be no spiritual leadership. And without some measure of humility, there can be no spiritual sensing.

Without intuition or spiritual sensing, there can be no spiritual leadership. And without some measure of humility, there can be no spiritual sensing. Although Collins doesn't suggest this, and I have no research basis for asserting it, my hunch is that this truth may be a root explanation for why the good-to-great companies were led by individuals distinguished by their humility. Perhaps these leaders were able to sense at a level simply not accessible to their more egotistical counterparts at the comparison companies. In humility, we may come to a stunning realization that how reality is fundamentally set up and how it works are dramatically different from what the arrogance of the human ego would allow us to perceive.

LEADING FROM A PLACE OF PEACE AND CLARITY

Spiritual leaders have discovered that, just as the eye of a hurricane is a place of calm, so it is possible to locate a stillness, clarity, or "centeredness" within, even when political storms or organizational tumult threaten to engulf. What this looks like in practice is well illustrated by an experience that Les Adelson had as a new superintendent of schools in South Pasadena, California.

A shooting took place during a football game in South Pasadena, and two students were wounded. Adelson was scheduled to meet with 700 angry parents and community members in an auditorium shortly after the shooting. Prior to the meeting, emotions swirled; it seemed that everyone had an opinion on how Adelson should handle the meeting. "People were yelling at me for 2 days, coming into my office and telling me what I should do," he later told me.

Just before the meeting, Adelson told his secretary he needed some time alone. He closed his office door and sat at his desk. In his words,

> This is the closest thing I've ever done to meditation. In retrospect, I think I might just call it reflection. And I've even teased that I felt like I had divine intervention. There was something that gave me strength and wisdom. When I sat quietly enough and long enough, it just started coming together. I sat at my computer and wrote a statement, which actually turned out to be a 10-minute speech. The comment I got after the meeting, which went incredibly well, was that it was a defining moment for me as a leader to the community. From that day forward I was treated differently. My board said, "Wow, we didn't know you had that in you." That was a very spiritual experience, really reaching down to the depths. (as quoted in Thompson, 2005b, p. 106)

In his remarks, Adelson acknowledged people's fears and set forth a plan to establish a broadly inclusive task force that would be charged with determining what was needed to move the community forward.

The key questions when confronted with a crisis may be these: *What is going on in my heart? What is my state of mind or consciousness?* And while there is an almost overwhelming temptation, when pressures intensify, to allow external events to define one's state of consciousness, it is possible to resist that temptation. It is possible because experience is far more mental than our senses and rationality would lead us to believe.

Evidence pointing to the mental nature of human experience is not entirely anecdotal. As surgeon and Yale professor Bernie Siegel (1986) has noted, "Unconditional love is the most powerful stimulant of the immune system" (p. 181). More recently, neuroscientists have reached similar conclusions concerning the relationship between compassion and immune system functions by studying practitioners of Buddhist meditation (Hall, 2003).

Consciousness of the Underlying Wholeness of People and Organizations

Each day, educational leaders encounter mountains of evidence suggesting that they are living and working in a world of fragmentation and conflict. The events, encounters, issues, and actions that make up any given day on the job feel like one disconnected thing after another. Educational leaders regularly see people and groups of people working at cross purposes when it was never their intention to do so. They "put out fires," go to meetings, answer countless e-mails, and struggle to implement externally imposed mandates and regulations.

Both spiritual traditions and contemporary scientific discoveries suggest that at a deep, invisible level, wholeness is the nature of reality itself, and that what we experience as fragmentation is an illusion or misperception. David Bohm was a leading 20th-century physicist and theorist who worked with Einstein and various pioneers of the quantum revolution. He was also inspired by mysticism and made contact with both J. Krishnamurti and the Dalai Lama. Bohm's book *Wholeness and the Implicate Order* (1980) includes the following observations:

> [F]ragmentation is now very widespread, not only throughout society, but also in each individual; and this is leading to a kind of general confusion of the mind, which creates an endless series of problems and interferes with our clarity of perception

so seriously as to prevent us from being able to solve most of them . . . some might say: "Fragmentation of cities, religions, political systems, conflict in the form of wars, general violence, fratricide, etc., are the reality. Wholeness is only an ideal, toward which we should perhaps strive." But this is not what is being said here. Rather, what should be said is that wholeness is what is real, and that fragmentation is the response of this whole to man's action, guided by illusory perception, which is shaped by fragmentary thought. In other words, it is just because reality is whole that man, with his fragmentary approach, will inevitably be answered with a correspondingly fragmentary response. So what is needed is for man to give attention to his habits of fragmentary thought, to be aware of it, and thus to bring it to an end. Man's approach to reality may then be whole, and so the response will be whole. (pp. 1, 9)

Wholeness, we are coming to learn, underlies reality. Therefore, when you're struggling with whole-school change or whole-system transformation, it helps to remember that as fragmented, or even dysfunctional, as that school or system appears on the surface, *its actual underlying reality is wholeness.* Here is how Stephanie Pace Marshall (2006), the founding president of the Illinois Mathematics and Science Academy, expresses it:

The whole system for the whole school for the whole classroom for the whole child is not some ever-beyond-our-reach ideal; it is what underlies the broken surface of misperception.

I believe we are in the midst of a silent yet discernable transformation of consciousness. Our cultural mind is slowly shifting from fragmentation and reductionism, expressed in excessive competition, unbridled acquisition, winning, short-term thinking, and isolated self-interest, to integration and interdependence—collaboration, shared purpose, and global sustainability. (p. 179)

From this perspective, the whole system for the whole school for the whole classroom for the whole child is not some ever-beyond-our-reach ideal; it is what underlies the broken surface of misperception. As consciousness awakens to the presence of the whole, then political, cultural, and structural obstacles lose some of their obstinacy, and the possibilities for educational advancement assume new tangibility and traction.

Make no mistake: Creating and sustaining this shift in consciousness is enormously difficult. We don't gain an inch against the obfuscation of fragmentation by chirping platitudes. As Peter Senge (Senge & Wheatley, 2002) has noted, "We're talking about real, 180-degree change—instead of trying to control everything, we're learning to align our intentions with emerging realities. This is a profound shift in our way of being" (p. 65). Yet when educational leaders who are spiritual practitioners have made this shift, they have found themselves thinking and acting in ways that feel profoundly natural, authentic. They not only feel more connected to reality itself, they also discern more of the actual wholeness of the schools or system they lead as well as the higher leverage that resides in wholeness.

WITHOUT SPIRITUAL DISCIPLINES THERE CAN BE NO SPIRITUAL LEADERSHIP

For educational leaders, rapid action is the fabric of the workday. The spiritual dimensions of educational leadership are scarcely discernable in the social upheaval and political turmoil aroused by fundamental reform. In such an environment, a spiritual perspective can only be gained through considerable discipline. As the educational leadership consultant John Morefield observes,

> Leadership is really hard. And educational leadership is only getting harder. You sure as hell don't do it for fame and fortune. The only reason I can see that people stick with it over time is because they have some sense of calling to do leadership work on behalf of children, and it comes from some deep well within them. I do a lot of work with folks on "How do you sustain this? How do you keep the fire lit? How do you avoid putting too many logs on the fire and making the fire smolder? How do you keep the spaces in between the logs so that flames can live? What are those spaces? What are the spaces for you? Do you have any? Do you fill your life up, leaving no space?"[1] The sustaining of one's well-being, one's health, is important; it allows deeply committed people to stay for the long haul. (as quoted in Thompson, 2005b, p. 40)

Morefield points out that the development of this kind of spiritual sustenance requires "sacred spaces," which must intentionally be created and preserved. "We have to take action to create inaction. . . . That inaction is not passive in the sense that there is work happening" (Thompson, 2005b, p. 40).

Spiritual practices accomplish two vital things: (1) renewal of energy and purpose and (2) fuller access to the true dimensions of the inner work that educational leaders engage in.

Okay, so what are some of these practices? The sources of spiritual nourishment and renewal, of course, can be highly individualistic. For many, it will involve some form of communion with their God. For others, it might involve ritualistic practices, prayer, or meditating on images that are significant for them. For still others, it might involve walking in the woods, jogging, writing in a journal, or finding ways of reconnecting to the passionate core of their values and beliefs. All of these various practices have the potential of being disciplines, if developed and honed through habitual and mindful practice. Some essential features of mindful practice follow.

Spiritual practices accomplish two vital things: (1) renewal of energy and purpose and (2) fuller access to the true dimensions of the inner work that educational leaders engage in.

Early Morning. Many spiritual practitioners have found the quiet of early morning to be an indispensable sanctuary for gaining spiritual ground. John Kammerud, superintendent of the Mauston (Wisconsin) School District, has developed the habit of listening to reflective music in his office for about 15 minutes at the start of each day. He reads the Bible or poetry before strenuous meetings in order to gain the sense of stillness and spiritual grounding (Thompson, 2005b, p. 41).

Early morning is not the only time for the exercise of spiritual habits, but for working professionals—especially if they have family or community obligations in the evenings—it is often the one time of day that is most easily protected and most naturally ripe for reflection.

Time. Anyone close to education knows that towering near the top of virtually every educator's list of factors that stall progress are time constraints. This is true for teachers and for educational leaders at all levels. Everything that meaningful educational practice demands takes time, whether it's developing collaborative relationships, engaging in professional development, or designing an accountability system. And it's not as though the ongoing demands that already seem to consume educators' every spare moment can be magically suspended.

Similarly, the discipline of spiritual leadership requires some of that same essential, scarce resource: time. "Making time to quiet myself and travel inward is difficult at times," observes Mark Bielang (2003), superintendent in Paw Paw, Michigan. "I find I have to schedule those moments of reflection" (p. 36).

Because the substance and influence of spirituality are hidden, it's especially hard to make time for spiritual practice. But there's an important paradox in spiritual practice that educational leaders would be wise not to ignore: While spiritual practice takes time, it also can have a liberating effect in relation to the imprisoning experience of time. Spiritual practitioners often have found that their discipline sets them free. The exercise of spiritual disciplines often results in increased inspiration and insight, and these can be time-savers.

Sacrifice. When a virtuoso musician or athlete takes our breath away by making an astonishing accomplishment look nearly effortless, we are seeing not just exceptional talent, but the fruits of sacrifice. The countless hours of practice that made the performance possible came, of course, at a steep price. More often than not, the individuals were willing to make the sacrifice because their love of the art or sport was greater than their love of what they were giving up in all those hours of practice. In addition, such sacrifice often extends beyond the individual to close family members, friends, and supporters. In fact, any devoted parent quickly becomes completely familiar with the taste of sacrifice.

Spirituality that is substantial and meaningful, spirituality that is something more than the occasional feel-good bromide, is born of sacrifice and is the fruit of persistent practice.

Persistence. Consistency of practice is essential if one's spirituality is to be meaningfully experienced and developed. In this sense, spiritual practices need to become habitual. At the same time, one must stay alert to ensure that habitual practices not become unthinking routines, in which the practitioner is simply jumping through a hoop of a different shape. The key is *persistently renewed mindfulness.*

Here we are talking about persistence in two different but ultimately interdependent ways. Each spiritual endeavor requires the spiritual practitioner's persistence. When we commence praying, studying, reflecting, writing, walking, or getting still, we will at times feel spiritually disconnected or apathetic. Just as there is resistance to change in education, there is also internal resistance to spiritual growth. If we always wait for a more inspired time for our spiritual practice, we will likely find that our procrastination has allied itself with that which resists our spiritual development. So don't delay, persist. Be dogged in seeking to reconnect with the source of purpose, meaning, inspiration, and spiritual grounding.

Long-term persistence opens our lives to dimensions that would otherwise remain concealed under materialism's garish and distracting surfaces.

We also need to be persistent over time in terms of regular practice across months, years, and decades. It's that long-term persistence that opens our lives to dimensions that would otherwise remain concealed under materialism's garish and distracting surfaces.

Compassion. Compassion is an important measure of spiritual authenticity, and it's essential to spiritual leadership for school reform. Why? Because educational change is disruptive, painful, and too complex not to be loaded with false starts and missteps. All of this is true not just for leaders but also for stakeholders throughout the system. When the status quo is disrupted and routines are shaken, people find themselves at an uncomfortable and risky distance from the familiar. Leaders who ignore this suffering undercut the foundational trust, openness, and ownership on which cultural and structural transformations must be built. A compassionate leader recognizes what fellow stakeholders are going through and communicates verbally and practically his or her rock-solid support.

Carol Johnson, superintendent in Memphis, Tennessee, has this to say:

> I think that religion is filled with examples of mercy. One of the things educational leaders can bring to their work is trying to operationalize that spiritual mercy in concrete ways. It's this ability to understand that part of being spiritually connected is understanding your imperfections well enough to be merciful

and patient with those who are imperfect. There have been times when my spiritual faith was the only thing that allowed me to forgive. (as quoted in Thompson, 2005b, p. 47)

Becky van der Bogert, superintendent in Winnetka, Illinois, came home on a Friday evening feeling frazzled and angry in the aftermath of a series of irate and sometimes threatening phone calls from parents and community members over a controversial staffing situation.

The next morning, she was still upset. Several staff members would soon be retiring, so van der Bogert turned her thoughts to a project relating to the retirement party, selecting wise and inspiring quotations and framing them for each retiree. As she worked on this project, taking in the spiritual import of the writings from which the quotations were drawn, her thoughts rose to a higher altitude—like an aircraft breaking through a dark cloud ceiling into sunlight.

"It put me on a totally different plane," she told me. "I felt almost soft toward the people who were threatening me" (as quoted in Thompson, 2005a, p. 29).

Van der Bogert realized that parents' concern for their children underlay the threats; as a mother, she could empathize with that. With this clearer and calmer perspective, she was able to develop a plan for addressing parents' concerns.

WILL YOU JOIN THE REVOLUTION?

> *Without a revolution in the sphere of human conscious-ness, nothing will change for the better in the sphere of our being as humans.*
>
> —Václav Havel[2]

According to Thomas Friedman (2005) and many other keen observers, we are living in the midst of a revolution. Globalization is dramatically shifting economies around the world, with enormous implications for the world in which our young people will be living and leading. Already, technologies connect American corporations to skilled workers in India, China, and elsewhere who work for wages that are a fraction of what American workers require if our standard of living is not to take a precipitous dive.

And, as the New Commission on the Skills of the American Workforce report, *Tough Choices or Tough Times* (2007), makes clear, avoiding tough times will require nothing less than revolutionizing our system of public education. Whether that revolution is

I have come to believe that the revolutionary changes now needed in our educational system can only be accomplished through the revolutionizing of human consciousness.

aligned with the commission's radical prescriptions or follows a different route, what is clear is that our current addiction to high-stakes-test–driven accountability is at complete odds with the rich array of disciplines and fields of inquiry that our students will need in order to prosper in the decades ahead.

I have come to believe that the revolutionary changes now needed in our educational system can only be accomplished through the revolutionizing of human consciousness. As Allison Phinney (2002) notes, "The most immediate task in these times may be to summon living, spirit-centered convictions among those who have leadership roles" (p. 250). Through the mindful exercise of spiritual practices, human consciousness can wake up and discover the true dimensions of educational leadership that result in cultures where students and teachers thrive and reach for new altitudes of learning.

NOTES

1. John Morefield explained to me that he drew the metaphor of the fire from a poem called "Fire" in *The Sea Accepts All Rivers and Other Poems,* by Judy Sorum Brown (Alexandria, VA: Miles River Press, 2000).

2. From Václav Havel, speech to the U.S. Congress, February 21, 1990.

REFERENCES

Bell, D. (2002). *Ethical ambition: Living a life of meaning and worth.* New York: Bloomsbury.

Bielang, M. T. (2003). Standing still in the wilderness. *The School Administrator, 60*(8), 36.

Bohm, D. (1980). *Wholeness and the implicate order.* New York: Routledge Classics.

Collins, J. (2001). *Good to great: Why some companies make the leap and others don't.* New York: Harper Business.

Friedman, T. (2005). *The world is flat: A brief history of the 21st century.* New York: Farrar, Straus and Giroux.

Hall, S. S. (2003, September 14). Is Buddhism good for your health? *The New York Times Magazine, 46–49.*

Marshall, S. P. (2006). *The power to transform: Leadership that brings learning and schooling to life.* San Francisco: Jossey-Bass.

New Commission on the Skills of the American Workforce. (2007). *Tough choices or tough times.* San Francisco: Jossey-Bass.

Phinney, A. W. (2002). The dynamic now—A poet's counsel. In B. S. Baudot (Ed.), *Candles in the dark: A new spirit for a plural world* (pp. 237–252). Manchester: New Hampshire Institute of Politics at Saint Anselm College.

Senge, P. M., & Wheatley, M. (2002). Changing how we work together. *Reflections, 3*(3), 63–67.

Sergiovanni, T. J. (1992). *Moral leadership: Getting to the heart of school improvement.* San Francisco: Jossey-Bass.

Siegel, B. S. (1986). *Love, medicine, and miracles.* New York: Harper & Row.

Spears, L. C. (Ed.). (1995). *Reflections on leadership: How Robert K. Greenleaf's theory of servant-leadership influenced today's top management thinkers.* New York: Wiley.

Stokley, F. (2002). What it means to be a spiritual leader. *The School Administrator, 59*(8), 48–50.

Thompson, S. (2005a, November). Habits of spiritually grounded leaders. *The School Administrator, 62*(10), 26–29.

Thompson, S. (2005b). *Leading from the eye of the storm: Spirituality and public school improvement.* Lanham, MD: Rowman & Littlefield Education.

Thompson, S. (2006, March 1). The importance of "reculturing." *Education Week, 25*(25), 30–31, 44.

Wheatley, M. (1999). *Leadership and the new science: Discovering order in a chaotic world.* San Francisco: Berrett-Koehler.

Wheatley, M. (2005). Foreword: The human spirit and school leadership. In S. Thompson, *Leading from the eye of the storm: Spirituality and public school improvement* (pp. ix–xiii). Lanham, MD: Rowman & Littlefield Education.

CHAPTER TEN

LEADERSHIP ON A TEETER-TOTTER

Balancing Rationality and Spirituality

TERRENCE E. DEAL

Top-performing organizations have high standards; they measure progress consistently and systematically. Achieving excellence has an equally vital existential pillar, however—one that is ethereal and hard to quantify, but with powerful and far-reaching effects. Attaining distinction demands bifocal leaders who can counterpoise rationality and spirituality. An overly logical organization lacks vigor; an overly zealous, spirit-driven enterprise often lacks rigor.

Imagine a playground teeter-totter or seesaw. Most of us can recall being on one with someone much heavier on the other end. When that happens, the teeter-totter loses its stable fulcrum point and is thrown out of balance. Equilibrium becomes impossible, spoiling the ups and downs that make a seesaw so much fun.

A similar problem presents itself when either rationality or spirituality weighs too heavily in an organization. Leadership on a seesaw is a balancing act. Some leaders seek to tighten things up, while others strive to set the spirit free. Too much influence in either direction means trouble.

Peoples Express was an airline started in the 1970s by Donald Burr. His was a zealous vision to create a revolutionary new enterprise with an exceptional spirit. His overall purpose was evangelistically ambitious: "[to] become the leading institution for change in the world" (Williams & Deal, 2003, p. 104). The route to this ambitious quest, as he saw it, was simple: Take care of your people; take care of customers. The main message was distilled into a focused slogan: "At Peoples Express, attitude is as important as altitude" (p. 108).

Some leaders seek to tighten things up, while others strive to set the spirit free. Too much influence in either direction means trouble.

At first, Burr's expansive dream flourished to the astonishment of everyone—most notably his competitors. With low fares and pleasant flights, Peoples Express quickly became a major player in the airline business. But its phenomenal success came too quickly. While its spirit was uniquely indomitable, its systems failed to keep pace. The company's computer technology was obsolete and its operating infrastructure neglected. These glitches paved the way for Peoples Express's competitors to make significant inroads. American Airlines, in particular, perfected "yield management," designating a percentage of seats on every flight to be sold at discount rates to match or undercut the fares of the lower-cost airline. Despite the fervent commitment of its founder and the intense dedication of highly motivated employees, Peoples Express succumbed to competitors whose technical systems were superior. The current travails of JetBlue may forecast a similar scenario unless the company upgrades its structure to match its spunk.

Home Depot represents the opposite side of the rationality/spirituality imbalance. The company, founded by Bernie Marcus and Arthur Blank, was renowned for its folksy ways, spirited pep rallies, decentralized operations, customer service, and the color orange. As is often the case with companies that experience rapid initial growth, sales started to wane 20 years after Home Depot was launched. Bob Nardelli, a top executive with General Electric, was brought in to tighten the ship. His agenda was clear: "Replace the old, sometimes random management style with new rigor."

At first, Nardelli's militaristic command-and-control approach worked. Profits and stock price soared. Then the bottom fell out. Home Depot, once an industry leader in customer satisfaction, dropped to last place—well below that of Lowe's, its chief competitor. A Web site with the title "Home Depot Sucks" created a public forum where angry customers could register their discontent. A former executive remarked, "My perception is that the mechanics are there. The soul isn't" (Grow, 2006). As Home Depot's fortunes fell, Nardelli plummeted from the darling of *Business Week* to a highly visible front-cover failure. His termination brought him a generous severance package, much to the chagrin of employees. Home Depot is now working to restore its spirit.

Either structural or spiritual disequilibrium damages performance. In the business world, harmony between the two pays off. Southwest Airlines, for example, tops most people's list of perennially successful organizations, even though it competes in a struggling sector of the economy. The company has high standards for short turnarounds, safety, customer service, and profitability. But the thriving enterprise also has an impeccable, and well-earned, reputation for engaging people's hearts as well as their heads and hands. Southwest employees are not just flying airplanes. Their higher calling—or ennobling purpose, as former CEO Herb Kelleher puts it—is to provide people with the freedom to fly. This means extending air travel to those who once did not have the means to attend a wedding or graduation, comfort a dying relative, or be present at a birth. To Southwest employees, work has meaning beyond a paycheck. Whatever their formal job—taking reservations, loading bags, or flying planes—people at Southwest are united in a common quest. The symmetry between rationality and spirituality is a prime factor in the company's success.

In business, from time to time, the balance between structure and spirit needs to be reviewed, and possibly renewed. Starbucks CEO Howard Schultz is not shy about expressing his desire for all his employees to pour their hearts into every cup of coffee they brew. But recently, the company's spirit has started to wane. The company's once sterling image has begun to erode. Rapid expansion and automating espresso machines have begun to water down what Schultz has called the "Starbucks Experience." A memo to top executives flagged the problem: "[Our] stores no longer have the soul of the past. . . . [I]t's time to get back to the core and make the changes necessary to evoke the heritage, the tradition, and the passion that we all have for the true Starbucks experience" (Gross, 2007).

So how do these comparisons apply to America's educational system? A common critique argues that schools should behave more like businesses. Buried in this critique is the implication that schools should become more rational. In pursuing this direction, unfortunately, we are gleaning illogical lessons from the wrong companies. As a result, the technical-spiritual teeter-totter has bottomed out off beam. Schools are out of whack because their souls have shriveled and their spirit has dampened, not simply because they lack rigorous standards or tangible results.

———————— ❧ ————————

Schools are out of whack because their souls have shriveled and their spirit has dampened, not simply because they lack rigorous standards or tangible results.

For decades, reforms in education have targeted goals, objectives, and standardized measures of performance. This barrage has undermined the ennobling purpose of teaching and learning. The commonly heard phrase "I'm just a teacher" is one symptom of what has happened. Creativity, building character, and learning how to work cooperatively with others have all been sacrificed to information-driven yardsticks that don't come close to capturing the true purpose of education. The time has come, in Howard Schultz's words, to evoke the heritage, the tradition, and the passion that have the power to restore the soul of American education.

How can this occur? The answer can be summed up in one word: leadership. For some time, schools have been overmanaged and under-led. Management is on the control-and-consequences end of the teeter-totter. Leadership, focusing on passion and purpose, is on the opposite end. The imbalance, which now favors management, has taken its toll on the spiritual underbelly of education. To regain the proper and necessary equilibrium between systems and soul, superintendents and principals at the local level need to focus less on the mechanics of instruction and more on the deeper meaning of teaching and learning. This will require attending more intensively to the historically validated symbolic mainstays of a caring and cohesive community: history, shared values and beliefs, heroic icons, ritual and ceremony, and stories. What has become a fleeting afterthought needs to become a top priority.

History. Where we have been shapes where we are and influences where we're headed. Herb Kelleher of Southwest Airlines credits the early struggles of launching a new venture with solidifying the strong core of values that sets the company apart from many of its competitors. Too often in schools, people have forgotten or forsaken their roots. The past—with its triumphs and travails, trials and errors—is a source of important lessons that are applicable to today's challenges. For instance, the principal of an elementary school was pleasantly surprised at the results of turning an hour and a half of the back-to-school orientation over to veteran teachers. They led everyone on a trip down memory lane, and it made a big difference in the attitudes of both the old-timers as well as the newcomers. Her conclusion: "There are two victims when the past is not shared. Those people who haven't a clue about the origins of traditions and ways— and those who know the roots and never get a chance to share old times with others."

Shared Values and Beliefs. The things we hold most dear and that we stand for can become a rallying point with the power to unify a group of people. These powerful intangibles can be expressed in symbols and slogans that everyone knows and agrees to live by rather than incomprehensible mission statements that no one understands or remembers. In one elementary school I know, the phrase "Every child a promise" speaks volumes about the true nature of the life and the work in that school. Contrast that with another school whose written philosophy adorns a hallway—but no one knows what it means.

When Lou Gerstner became the CEO of a struggling IBM, he was charged with setting a new course. His reputation as a hard-headed, results-driven manager suggested that he would steer the company in a radically more structured, goal-oriented direction. Indeed, in his first press conference, he stressed, "The last thing IBM needs is a vision."

Very quickly, however, Gerstner discovered that IBM had drifted from a vision and set of values that historically had made the company one of the most admired in the world. His main job became one of restoring and revitalizing IBM's soul:

> My deepest culture-change goal was to induce IBMers to believe in themselves again—to believe that they had the ability to determine their own fate, and that they already knew what they needed to know. It was to shake them out of their depressed stupor and remind them of who they were. (Bolman & Deal, 2006, p. 182)

In an organization infused with spirit, people know what they are doing and why, and they believe that their efforts make a significant difference.

Heroes. Many people think of heroes only as those who fearlessly charge enemy bunkers or arrive on white horses to clean up Dodge City. Another way to look at heroic figures, however, is to focus on individuals who exemplify cultural values. These ordinary people are living emblems or icons because their exploits model ideals that have the power to inspire others. In the maintenance department of a large university, a new engineer asked for a list of the department's values. His supervisor responded, "You don't need a written list of values. Just watch what we do."

Teachers, for example, are more significant for who they are and what they do than for what they teach. Their everyday behavior radiates lessons or signposts that students absorb.

Teachers, for example, are more significant for who they are and what they do than for what they teach. Their everyday behavior radiates lessons or signposts that students absorb. Ask anyone to identify his or her heroes, and the list is sure to include one (or several) teachers.

Just as important, heroes have the moral authority to anoint others whose virtues represent what an organization treasures. The principal of a certain elementary school, for example, is well known for her constant drive to achieve excellence, to push herself well beyond what even she thought she could do. Her persistent striving to better herself models for others the school's motto, "Reach for Excellence." She also goes to great lengths to recognize others who push themselves to new heights. When students demonstrate remarkable growth, she convenes the entire school community—including parents—to witness the student's induction into the Hall of Fame. The Hall is one of the school's hallways which has taken on special meaning. The principal announces the student's special accomplishment and paints his or her hand with paint. The student then slaps the wall with a vigorous high five, and the principal writes the student's name beside the handprint. The colorful hallway wall vividly symbolizes the school's commitment to constantly striving to improve, and the public anointment of heroes sets examples for others to emulate.

Ritual and Ceremony. Eons ago, religious leaders realized that ritual and ceremony expressed and buttressed the beliefs that bind the faithful flock together. Changing the traditional liturgy usually splinters a community and dampens the faith. The Catholic Church felt this impact when Mass was switched from the traditional Latin to more familiar English. In retrospect, the words were not as important as the tradition itself. As Richard Rodriguez (1982) laments in *Hunger of Memory,*

> I cannot expect the liturgy—which reflects and cultivates my faith—to remain what it was. I will continue to go to the English mass. I will go because it is my liturgy. I will, however, often recall with nostalgia the faith I have lost. (p. 107)

In too many contemporary secular organizations, leaders fail to realize that a meaningful workplace also hinges on ritual and ceremony. These symbolic occasions knit an organization together and remind people of the special sentiments, hopes, and destiny they share. Too often these important intangibles lie dormant, failing to beckon for public appreciation the awe-inspiring spirit that captures people's hearts.

To illustrate, on a flight from Chicago to Nashville, several soldiers returning from Operation Desert Storm were seated in coach class. The flight attendant asked first-class passengers if they would mind trading places with the men in uniform. All agreed, and the soldiers were moved up to the front of the plane. As the passengers disembarked upon arrival, they walked through the concourse toward a sea of yellow ribbons and flowers on the other side of security. A little girl with a yellow bow in her hair bolted through the security checkpoint, ran down the concourse, and jumped into her daddy's arms. The usual clamor of the airport fell silent. A faint murmur rippled through the crowd, and without prompting everyone joined in singing "God Bless America." The soldiers received an ovation. A group of diverse strangers was magically transformed into a unified band of Americans. The lesson: shared sentiments lie just beneath the surface of everyday life. Ritual and ceremony have the power to draw those sentiments to the forefront for public display and appreciation.

Rituals are routine with a deeper meaning. "Rituals reveal values at their deepest level. . . . [People] express in ritual what moves them most, and since the form of expression is conventionalized and obligatory, it is the values of the group that are revealed" (Moore & Meyerhoff, 1977, p. 32). Physicians scrub for 7 minutes before a surgery, even though germs are destroyed by modern germicides in 30 seconds. The scrub prepares the surgical team to execute a delicate procedure successfully. As we observed in the old TV series *Hill Street Blues*, roll call for police officers is full of playful jabbing and jocularity. Its deeper purpose is to help officers face life-and-death situations on the streets. As Sarge would always conclude, " . . . and be careful out there."

Celebrations are special occasions intended to put values and beliefs on display. The shared spirit warms the heart and reaffirms the soul. Mary Kay Cosmetics is renowned for its lavish seminars with pink Cadillacs and diamond bumblebee awards. Beneath the glitter is the unique "You Can Do It" spirit that has made the company so successful. The event draws beauty consultants together, reminds them of what the company is all about, and sends them on their way with renewed energy and commitment.

At a major university, a fund-raising campaign gave alumni an opportunity to share the highlights of their experience as students. Nearly all mentioned specific faculty members. At the end of a highly successful fund drive, the board of trustees hosted an evening for those professors who had been singled out for special mention. At the end of a fabulous dinner, the board gave the professors a standing ovation. The implicit message was clear: at this university, teaching is a high priority.

Without meaningful rituals and frequent celebrations, an organization can become sterile and lose its way.

Without meaningful rituals and frequent celebrations, an organization can become sterile and lose its way.

Stories. Long before the Information Revolution and the advent of sophisticated technology, people communicated through narratives or stories. In answering a question, a common response might be, "Let me tell you a story." Today, a questioner typically might be encouraged to, "Look it up on Google." Google is a splendid resource for getting information—but it is not a replacement for a good story. We remember stories. Embedded in the narrative are important lessons and triggers for our emotions. It has been said that

God created people because he loves stories. In this light, it seems ironic that universities often discourage the telling of "war stories" in the classroom. Stories transform both the storyteller and the listeners and transport them to another dimension of living.

The late Jim Valvano, one-time basketball coach at North Carolina State, was diagnosed with terminal cancer. Before he passed away, there was a widely attended special tribute in his honor. Just before the event, Valvano was reportedly so ill that it wasn't clear whether he would make it through the evening. During the course of the occasion, he was given an opportunity to make some remarks. He began by giving the audience some advice for living a good life and then switched to telling a story.

Valvano recalled his first coaching job at Rutgers University. Predictably, he wanted his career to get off on a winning note. His idol was Vince Lombardi, legendary coach of the Green Bay Packers football team. He learned that before his first game, Lombardi had created a suspenseful moment by not showing up at the locker room until one minute before his players were to take the field. He forcefully banged open the door, looked each player in the eye, and then said, "Gentlemen, we will be successful if you attend to three things: your family, your religion, and the Green Bay Packers." The Packers proceeded to trounce the opposition and went on to a winning season.

Valvano decided before Rutgers' first game to emulate his idol. He waited outside the locker room until one minute before game time. Then he tried to bang open the door just as Lombardi had done. It didn't open. He almost broke his arm. A player opened the door, and Valvano fell on the floor. His players helped him up. He paced back and forth, looking each player in the eye, rubbing his throbbing arm. Then he said in as forceful a voice as he could muster under the circumstances, "Gentlemen, we will be successful this season if you pay attention to three things and three things only: your family, your religion, and the Green Bay Packers."

As Valvano told the story, he was transformed into an energetic, cancer-free human being, and his audience was with him all the way. The story was not about his first success. It was a vivid account of his first failure. In one magic moment, Valvano had displayed the charm that had captured the hearts of so many people.

Schools are among this nation's most storied organizations. They are chockfull of sidesplitting tales as well as poignant stories that warm the heart. It is rewarding to witness what happens when teachers and administrators swap yarns. Like Jim Valvano, they are transformed. They become more animated and more emotional. They laugh at the humorous tales and cry over the moving narratives.

Stories carry subtle cultural messages that seep into our pores and are tattooed on our hearts and souls. Teaching can be a supremely frustrating line of work. The dedication and enthusiasm that teachers pour into educating young people often does not produce immediate tangible results. With so little short-term feedback, teachers can begin to wonder if their efforts make much difference. Only much later—if at all—will they really know. A belated thank-you from a former student or hearing a good story from another teacher can restore faith and reignite a teacher's flagging energy.

A high school teacher, Mr. Smith, recalled his experience with a former student. The boy's mother was a prostitute, his father a drug dealer. Mr. Smith took an interest in the student and did what he could to cultivate and support the student's special talents. Years later, the student, now a successful businessman, came by Mr. Smith's house with a wrapped package. In the box was a platinum Rolex watch. Mr. Smith tried to explain that he could not accept such an expensive present. The gift-giver persisted. "Mr. Smith," he said, "you need to understand your invaluable contribution to my life. Everyone but you thought I was garbage. You believed in me and encouraged me. I can never thank you enough. I want you to have this watch. Besides, I inscribed it to you." On the back of the watch was etched, "To Mr. Smith with gratitude and love, Johnny."

Mr. Smith was fortunate. His career choice was validated as he neared retirement. He had made a difference in one student's life. And through the telling of the story, other teachers receive the benefits secondhand. It's something to hold onto as people age in a profession where the results of one's labor are often elusive. Think of the chilling alternative lamented by Frank McCourt (2005) in *Teacher Man:*

I had an English teacher, Miss Smith, who really inspired me. I'll never forget dear old Miss Smith. She used to say that if she reached one child in her forty years of teaching it would make it all worthwhile. She'd die happy. The inspiring teacher then fades into gray shadows to eke out her days on a penny-pinching pension, dreaming of the one child she might have reached. Dream on teacher. You will not be celebrated. (pp. 4–5)

Special narratives capture the essence of the teaching profession and everyone can delight in their telling and retelling. In recent years, scads of books on storytelling have been published in the business literature. We need a similar resurrection of a powerful means of enhancing spirituality in the field of education.

> Remember only this one thing. The stories people tell have a way of taking care of them. If stories come to you, care for them. And learn to give them away where they are needed. Sometimes a person needs a story—more than food to stay alive. That is why we put these stories in each other's memories. This is how people care for themselves.
>
> —Barry Lopez (from *Crow and Weasel,* 1990)

Without doubt, educational administrators today are overloaded with important things to be done and pressing problems to be solved. But most of these vexing management challenges are on the lower, rational end of an already out-of-kilter teeter-totter. What happens, as a result, is that the higher-order virtues of spirituality receive short shrift. To redeem the soul of American education, we need leaders who will step forward and give more attention to the fabric of intangibles—history, values and beliefs, ritual and ceremony, and stories—that breathe heart and meaning into any organization.

One of the vexing challenges of leadership is figuring out what is going on, sizing up a situation to determine the right thing to do. Our research (Bolman & Deal, 2006) probes into how leaders think, the way they make sense when faced with messy predicaments. Invariably,

Effective leadership depends mostly on a genuine feel for the intangibles that infuse organizations with meaning and soul.

they rely on individual or rational lenses. They are uncomfortable with politics and have trouble grasping subtle symbolic cues. Yet effective leadership depends mostly on a genuine feel for the intangibles that infuse organizations with meaning and soul. Moving forward in education will require a significant shift in mindset among both administrators and teachers. It's a crucial step we must take to regain what we have let slip away from us.

This doesn't mean that we must sacrifice standards and accountability. It means *balancing* them with passion and purpose. The pressing issue today is not improving test scores. It is reviving the spirit of education, and restoring hope and faith in the deeper value that schools offer to the lives of young people. As Tracy Kidder (1989) so eloquently summed it up in *Among School Children,*

> [Educators] put snags in the river of children passing by, and over the years, they redirect hundreds of lives. Many people find it easy to imagine webs of malevolent conspiracy in the world, and they are not always wrong. But there is an innocence that conspires to hold humanity together, and it is made up of people who can never fully know the good that they have done. (p. 313)

That intangible good is being eclipsed by an overly constricted version of what education is all about. Restoring parity requires either reducing the emphasis on standards and testing, which only policy makers can do, or giving more weight to the influences of spirituality and to the responsibility of educational leaders at the local level. If we don't do something now to correct the imbalance in our schools, we will reap some very costly consequences in the near future. It is a terrible price that our nation cannot afford to pay. By giving more heft to spirituality in schools, all of our hearts and souls will be enriched.

REFERENCES

Allison, M. (2007, March 14). Starbucks must find lost "soul," Schultz says. *Seattle Times.* Available online at http://seattletimes.nwsource .com/html/businesstechnology/2003586922_starbucks24.html.

Bolman, L. G., & Deal, T. E. (2006). *The wizard and the warrior: Leading with passion and power* San Francisco: Jossey-Bass.

Gross, D. (2007, March 4). Starbucks' "Venti" problem *Los Angeles Times.* Available at http://www.newscloud.com/read/Starbucks_venti_problem.

Grow, B. (2006, March 6). Renovating Home Depot. *Business Week.*

Kidder, T. (1989). *Among school children.* Boston: Houghton Mifflin

Lopez, B. (1990). *Crow and weasel.* San Francisco: North Point Press.

McCourt, F. (2005). *Teacher man.* New York: Scribner.

Moore, S. F., & Myerhoff, B. G. (1977). *Secular ritual.* Assen/Amsterdam: Van Gorcum.

Rodriguez, R. (1982). *Hunger of memory.* Boston: D. R. Godine

Williams, R. G., & Deal, T. E. (2003). *When opposites dance: Balancing the manager and the leader within.* Palo Alto, CA: Davies-Black.

INDEX

CORWIN PRESS

The Corwin Press logo—a raven striding across an open book—represents the union of courage and learning. Corwin Press is committed to improving education for all learners by publishing books and other professional development resources for those serving the field of PreK–12 education. By providing practical, hands-on materials, Corwin Press continues to carry out the promise of its motto: **"Helping Educators Do Their Work Better."**

The HOPE Foundation logo stands for Harnessing Optimism and Potential Through Education. The HOPE Foundation helps to develop and support educational leaders over time at district- and state-wide levels to create school cultures that sustain all students' achievement, especially low-performing students.

The American Association of School Administrators, founded in 1865, is the professional organization for more than 13,000 educational leaders across America and in many other countries. AASA's mission is to support and develop effective school system leaders who are dedicated to the highest quality public education for all children.